YOUR MONEY – YOUR LIFE

First published in 2007 by
CURRACH PRESS
55A Spruce Avenue, Stillorgan Industrial Park,
Blackrock, Co. Dublin

www.currach.ie

1 3 5 4 2

Cover by sin é design
Origination by Richard Parfrey
Printed by Betaprint, Bluebell Industrial Estate, Dublin 12

ISBN: 978-1- 85607-947-1

The author has asserted his moral rights

Whilst every effort has been made to ensure accuracy, the author and publishers can accept no legal or other liability for any information or advice given. It is advisable, in all cases, to seek independent legal advice.

Your Money – Your Life

Liam Croke

CURRACH
PRESS

Contents

1

WHY WE ARE IN DEBT

Every day we are bombarded by marketing messages. We are offered zero percent finance, buy now pay later, interest-only mortgages, pre-approved loans – to mention but a few. Our credit card limits are increased without our even asking. Figures released recently show that we are accepting these offerings: in the past two years personal debt in the Republic of Ireland has increased by a staggering €118.2 billion.

Statistics from the Central Bank has shown that most of this increased debt has come by way of term loans and overdrafts. Personal credit trebled from 48% of our disposable income in 1995 to 132% ten years later.

This rapid accumulation of personal debt has made many people vulnerable in their ability to meet their loan commitments, particularly should interest rates rise further or if they go through periods of unemployment or illness. However, there seems to be no end in sight and our insatiable appetite to use someone else's money to buy goods (that is, the bank's) simply means that our debt is going to continue to rise in the years ahead.

For many of us this is a situation that has developed over time and one that we feel we have little control over. Most worrying of all is that we do not know how to get ourselves out of the situation we are in. Before we can tackle our debts or overspending problems, we first have to admit that a problem exists and find out why we got so heavily into debt in the first place.

Here are some of the factors which, I believe, have

contributed to our current debt problems.

THE COST OF LIVING

We are all aware that Ireland is a very expensive country to live in (the second most expensive in the EU) and the cost of living is increasing more quickly than at any time in recent years. According to the Central Statistics Office, as of December 2006 inflation was 4.9%, with prices rising faster than at any time since 2002.

In the past number of months we have seen increases in the following sectors:

Education	up 4.9%
Transport	up 3.4%
Alcohol/tobacco	up 1.1%
Housing/water/gas/electricity/fuel	up 16.1%
Restaurants/hotels	up 3.9%

We have all read the headlines in the national newspapers claiming that Ireland is a 'graveyard for consumers'. We can all identify with these claims on a personal level given that we seem to be spending more and more each week/month on the most basic of items just to keep our homes running.

These increases have an obvious effect on our disposable income: our salaries are not increasing by as much as goods are so we have a problem and we have to bridge this shortfall in some way. Using overdrafts, credit cards and personal loans is a way of doing it.

If you were to go back over your current account transactions for the past number of months you will notice that the amount debited from your account each week to pay your groceries, for example, has increased each month. You are not buying any more items; it is just that goods are becoming more expensive. You don't even have to look back over your account to recognise this, you know it already. It might be only an extra €10 or €20 each week but over a twelve-month period that means an extra €1,000 from your pocket. Later in the book I will deal with how to shop smarter and give you tips that will actually help to save you money.

Figures released recently by the Central Statistics Office show that some food prices have risen by as much as 16%, even after the much publicised abolition of the Groceries Order, whereby the government lifted the ban on below-cost selling over twelve months ago. Groceries are just a simple and obvious example where we notice these increases but what about health costs rising by 4.4% in 2006 – nearly a third more expensive than in 2002 – doctors' fees up 7% from the previous year in 2006, dental costs up 6.6% and so on.

So out of necessity many of us have had to take on additional debt just to get by. This is the worst kind of debt you can have, but don't worry, even though prices are increasing every other day I will show you how to deal with this without having to take on debt. Simply changing your attitude to money, becoming a smarter shopper, taking control of your income, eliminating unnecessary expenditure and managing your money better will counteract the effects of price increases.

Poor Money Management

If you do not know what your fixed monthly outgoings are – for example your mortgage repayment, car-loan repayment, home-, health- and life-insurance premium – or when they are debited from your account, and if you do not know when and on what you spend the rest of your money each month, you have no idea where your money is going and you are looking for trouble.

Let me ask homeowners reading this book a question. Who is your house insured with? How much do you pay each month? When is it debited from your account? I suspect that very few readers will know the answer off the top of their heads. Do you know how much you spend on heating, take-aways, lunches, clothing, groceries, membership subscriptions, satellite TV...?

You will be surprised, perhaps shocked, if you take the time to sit down and analyse how you are spending your money each month. We all complain that by the middle of the month we have little or no money in our account and wonder where it has gone. It hasn't mysteriously vanished: it has gone on servicing your monthly loan commitments, some to pay your household utilities with the remainder going on those variable items such as entertainment, baby sitters, school expenses, topping up your phone credit, clothing, haircuts, DVDs and so on. Some of it, I hope, has even gone towards savings.

Most people know how much income they earn and how much is lodged to their account each month. It's easy we get a payslip showing the amount. We also know for sure the date it arrives in our account. *What we don't know is how much of that money is not ours to keep.* We are spending money that we don't have, which results in our becoming overdrawn and missing loan repayments – and all because we are not managing our finances properly.

I will outline in the next chapter how we can manage our money better each week/month. It starts with planning and this is no more difficult then writing down your income and expenditure each month and reconciling the two.

You will be surprised when you start to 'micro-manage' your money how empowered and enlightened you become. Then you start making smarter decisions about when and where you spend your money.

AVAILABILITY OF CREDIT

If you window-shop or browse at the weekend you will notice that many different kinds of shops such as furniture stores, jewelers and home-entertainment outlets now offer you the opportunity to buy goods through their in-house finance schemes. No need for cash, they will arrange the finance for you. It couldn't be more simple: fill out a few forms, provide them with some personal information and away you go. The enticement to purchase immediately rather than save and then buy is just too great an offer for many of us to pass up.

For example, we see fifty-inch televisions, Rolex watches –items we would not buy even if we had the money in savings because they are just too expensive. However, they are now within our grasp because we are being offered so-called cheap credit and easy repayment plans by a whole host of finance houses.

Many of us go into shops with no intention of buying anything but then we enter a zombie-like trance. We utter to ourselves the words '0% finance, no repayments for twelve months, €10 per week' and come out thirty minutes later having bought something we probably didn't need or want in the first place.

Hands up anyone who has received a letter from their bank or credit-card company advising them that they have been 'pre-approved' for a loan, or that their credit limit has been increased. You almost feel you have won something and are delighted with the bank's offering. You promise yourself, of course, that you will never use the credit, but in reality you will find an excuse to put it to some use at some stage. You might upgrade your perfectly good car or buy those new golf clubs you use five times a year.

Just because money (someone else's money) is dangled in front of you doesn't mean you have to use it!

Keeping Up with the Joneses

Many of us still have that sense of having to 'keep up with the Joneses'. The problem is, of course, that the Joneses can afford their trappings of luxury and the lifestyle they have.

Why are we obsessed with having to show our friends or family that money is not a problem for us when the reality may be different? You don't have to have a 2007 car, a holiday home abroad or throw your money around on a night-out to impress people. If this is why you have money problems you may have other issues you need to deal with first. Of course we want to enjoy life and buying new and expensive items gives us a sense of satisfaction, achievement and pleasure but don't live beyond your means to get them.

Money problems can be the deep-rooted cause of people falling ill. Acute anxiety is caused by worrying about how they are going to pay their bills and pay off their loans. Be smart, readjust your lifestyle if needs be. Who do you think sleeps better at night? Someone with savings and money in their account but a car that is a few years old parked in their drive or their next-door neighbour who has an expensive new car but no savings and very little in their account?

UNEMPLOYMENT

This is an unfortunate reason to be in debt and one that is perhaps beyond our control. It is happening more and more frequently though.

If you are suddenly made redundant it may take you a number of weeks or even months to find alternative employment that suits your particular skillset. In the interim your redundancy payment will be used to replace your previous earned income and will be quickly eroded. Some people may even have to borrow from family members until they return to work because they have no savings to call upon.

When you do find a new job, it may mean a reduction in income from what you previously earned so it is vital to adjust to your new situation, be it temporary or permanent.

LITTLE OR NO SAVINGS

The easiest way to avoid having to take on additional debt is to anticipate the bills that arrive every month or two. The best way to prepare for extra expenditure at Christmas time or to fund that annual holiday abroad is the old-fashioned method of savings.

Between 2001 and 2002 1.1 million Irish people began saving through the state-sponsored Special Savings Incentive Account (SSIA) scheme. Apparently as many as 78% of those taking part in the scheme were saving on a regular basis for the first time. The government bonus of 25% was fantastic but do we need to have our arms twisted to encourage us to start saving?

Having the comfort of savings gives us a cushion in the case of unforeseen events such as redundancy, illness or divorce. If we had savings to call on these events would not give rise to immediate financial hardship – the hardship that occurs as a result of increasing our level of debt.

I always hear people ask, 'How can I save if I have no money?' You will find a way. It doesn't matter how small or big the amount is, it is about getting into the savings habit and putting funds aside on a regular basis. It will quickly add up: just ask those who contributed to the SSIA scheme.

SEPARATION AND DIVORCE

More and more of us are doing it, and some even more than once!

Apart form the emotional strain caused by separation and divorce, there can be a heavy financial burden placed on those who are embarking on this course of action.

The loss of a second income, legal costs, paying maintenance, looking for a deposit to purchase another property, raising money so that you can buy your ex-spouse out of their share of your property – all these can contribute to an enormous increase in our level of personal debt.

Many people now find themselves having to return to work after a long absence because of becoming separated or divorced. They no longer have another income to rely on and have to start earning again in order to pay their mortgage and other expenses. They may also need to raise finance to purchase a car or arrange funds to pay for childcare for when they return to work.

All these changes in their personal circumstances may lead to an increased level of borrowing and debt.

Financial Illiteracy

There is a considerable number of people who just do not understand how money works, how it can grow, how and why we should have savings put aside for that rainy day. Worst of all they do not understand the value of money. Many of us are not taught about money in school, our parents may not have explained it to us when we were young, so we are ignorant about its workings.

This is a poor excuse: you are responsible for your life and your money. Collecting and increasing debt can be incredibly expensive and complicated to rectify.

The Irish Financial Regulator has published numerous papers on personal finance and is at pains to inform and advise people on the various products that are available in the marketplace and how they work.

We all know the advertisement on the TV where someone say, 'I don't know what a tracker mortgage is?' or 'I don't understand APR'. Well, if you are like the person in that advertisement, start educating yourself and get in control of your finances.

There are many other contributing factors to our increasing debt problems: for example, gambling, the death of a spouse, accident or illness, failed business ventures. However most people can identify with the points outlined in the last few pages: a combination of a number of these is probably what got us where we are today.

Enough of the causes – let's start dealing with the solutions.

2

FOCUS ON YOUR SITUATION

Getting into debt and increasing the amount owed on your credit card, overdraft or credit union loan is an easy thing to do; getting out of debt and clearing those loans is a much greater challenge, as we all know. Many people are oblivious of the amount of debt they have until one day they realise that they are facing a major problem: there isn't enough money to meet their loan obligations and they cannot fund their day-to-day living expenses.

Some people do know that their debt is increasing all the time, particularly at periods like Christmas, birthdays, holiday time, but they feel they cannot do anything about it or do not know where to go for advice, so they bury their head in the sand, hoping the problem will miraculously go away. This will, of course, only make matters a whole lot worse. People with debt problems or those who feel that they may be heading that way should take stock of their situation now. The sooner people realise this, the sooner they can put a plan in place and get out of the situation they are in.

Money is an uncomfortable topic for us to discuss and we are often at pains not to talk to anybody about it – including our bank manager or even our partner. It is essential that couples discuss their financial situation as each may have a different opinion as to what should be done with their money. Only by talking to each other will each get an understanding of what the other's attitude to finance is. Avoiding the subject will only lead to conflict as your debt grows and one person starts to blame the other for the situation they are in. So start communicating with each other!

THE TWO TYPES OF DEBT

We all typically have two types of debt.

The first is our mortgage which is a long-term debt secured on our principal private residence. Those who purchase investment properties will also have a mortgage secured on that buy-to-let property. A mortgage is often referred to as 'good debt' particularly if the value of your property is rising faster than what the mortgage is costing you.

Property values are now as frequent a topic of conversation as the weather and given how substantially they have increased over the past number of years is it any wonder? Remember that regardless how much your property may be worth on paper you will only see a financial benefit from it if you sell your home and repay the mortgage in full or in part. Unless we win the national lottery this is highly unlikely for most of us.

Our second type of debt is *unsecured borrowings* and they come in the form of:

- Credit cards
- Credit union loans
- Holiday loans
- Store credit card loans
- Furniture loans
- Car loans
- Computer loans
- Student loans (we may still be paying
  back years after we graduate)

These types of loan tend to be short term in nature, typically up to five years in duration. The rate of interest charged on the above loans can be very high, ranging from 8–18%. It is this short-term debt that is the cause of many people's problems and if it was brought under control, our disposable income would increase, our savings increase, our attitude to further borrowing change and our quality of life improve.

I read recently that in the UK 60% of illnesses suffered by people can be linked to money worries. So it is in all our interests to meet this problem head on and deal with it now, not tomorrow or next week but right now.

SO WHAT DO YOU DO?

STOP BORROWING MONEY

It may seem an obvious answer but this is your staring point: no more borrowings. You have got to stop making matters worse so before you make plans to tackle your existing debt, stop accumulating new debt.

This does not simply mean that you stop going to your local bank or credit union for top-up loans. It means removing what credit you currently have at your disposable, that is, your credit card and the large overdraft that you constantly make use of. Remove that temptation to use them now: cut up your credit card and reduce your overdraft limit.

MAKE A COMMITMENT

Do not decide that you are going to tackle your debt if you are not 100% committed to doing so. How many times have you decided to do this in the past and ended up not following through? You will only be successful if you commit to your plan.

You can start immediately by not living beyond your means. This involves:

- Not buying unnecessary items
- Paying with cash as much as possible
- Not buying what you don't need
- Watching out for 'bargains'

KNOW WHEN A BARGAIN IS A WASTE OF MONEY

Let me give you an example of a client of mine who thought he had just purchased a 'bargain'. He was browsing one Sunday afternoon with his wife when they happened upon a furniture store. In they went for a look and after five minutes they both spotted a lovely item of furniture at a reduced price. The normal price was €1,200 but for one day only the price was €1,000. Let me point out by the way that the couple did not need this item of furniture as the one they had at home was in perfect condition but the lure of (a) the discount and (b) the offer to finance the purchase with no repayments for twelve months was too much temptation for them both. They purchased the item and off they went delighted with themselves.

When they asked me recently to arrange a remortgage for them as cashflow was running tight, they wanted the loan that they had arranged to buy this piece of furniture to be consolidated with other debts they had. I noticed from the credit agreement that they had arranged the finance over a four-year period at a rate of 15.8%. The total payback for this loan was going to be €1,350. So the item they bought for €1,000 was going to cost them €1,350 greater than the cost of the item before its reduction. Not such a bargain after all.

This is a problem for many people nowadays: credit is too widely available and it is all too easy to purchase items that would previously have been beyond our means. What did people do in the past? They saved the money first and then bought. Why don't we do this? Are our kids noticing this and will they follow in our footsteps? I certainly hope not.

END UNNECESSARY SPENDING
By ending unnecessary expenditure I mean:

- changing where you buy your foodstuffs
- making your own lunch
- stopping paying for anything you neither need nor use, for example gym/golf membership
- shopping around for cheaper insurance
- bringing back your DVDs on time

- cancelling your digital TV subscription (sorry guys)

All these actions will help to increase the amount of income left over each month and help towards eliminating your debt. They are very much personal decisions and you have to decide what your number one priority is: being debt-free as fast as possible, or continuing each month to spend your money on items that support your current lifestyle.

CHECK ON YOUR SAVINGS

Having savings that are earning little or nothing in interest while paying 8–18% on borrowed money makes no sense whatsoever. For example, if you have €6,000 on deposit earning 4% in interest and €6,000 on your credit card which is being charged at 18% use those savings immediately to clear your credit card debt.

However, I would always encourage people to have some level of savings on deposit: what I call an 'emergency fund'. This would come into its own in the event of an unforeseen occurrence such as losing your job, suffering an accident or illness. I will deal with the emergency fund in more detail on pages 36-7 and 81-3.

ATTITUDE TO DEBT

Many psychologists believe that we formulate our attitudes to most things by the age of six. I firmly believe that how we deal with money and arrange our finances is down to having the right attitude. Some young people develop this attitude at a very early stage in life, that is when their parents educate them about the value of money, the importance of having savings and so on. They quickly find out how satisfying it is to save and purchase something with their own money and realise that the item bought is then appreciated so much more. This type of person continues with this mindset as they grow up. Saving money each week or month becomes second nature to them: it is just a good habit that started when they were young. These people may remember the words of their parents: 'Don't buy something that you can't afford to pay for.' Financial security may become very important to those who were reared with very little money and they tend to be conservative with investments and in the way they spend their money.

Of course you don't have to have been brought up in a savings culture or have had very little money when you were young to have the right attitude to spending and saving money. While this background may help, anyone can develop and change their attitude later in life.

Here are some questions now that I want you to answer honestly, just for yourself, and which may uncover exactly what your attitude to debt and spending is and whether you are financially self-destructive?

1. *Can you tell me who your present mortgage provider is, what you repay each month, what rate of interest you are being charged and whether your mortgage is fixed or variable?*
a. Yes of course I can.
b. Not really sure but have an idea.
c. No, not a clue.

2. *Can you confirm who your home insurance provider is, and how much do you pay each month?*
a. Yes.
b. Not exactly but I know where the insurance policy is and can find out.
c. No idea.

3. *Can you write down a list of your fixed monthly outgoings and tell me when each will be debited from your account?*
a. Yes I can, no problem.
b. I would have a good stab at it.
c. Ask my wife/husband.

4. *You are in a shop and you see something you want to purchase. You open your wallet/purse and you have the cash to pay for it and a credit card as well. Do you?*
a. Pay cash.
b. Use cash or the credit card, depending on the balance owed at the time.
c. Use the credit card and promise yourself you will pay the card bill with that money in your pocket when the bill arrives a month later.

5. *You're shopping for a car and ready to wheel and deal. Do you check with several lenders and see who is the cheapest? Go to your local bank and ask them to arrange finance for you? Or use the car dealership's in-house finance offering?*
a. Check with several lenders first.
b. Use your own bank.
c. Let someone in the car dealership arrange *finance* as you haven't time to do it yourself.

6. *Which if these best describes your habit for paying your monthly credit card bill?*
a. Always on time. You never have an amount outstanding.
b. A bit over plus the minimum payment each and every month.
c. You pay the minimum amount due, sometimes not until after a reminder.

7. *Do you know what interest rate you are currently earning on your savings held on deposit with your bank or credit union?*
a. Yes.
b. I have an idea.
c. What savings?

8. *You see that first Christmas advertisement on television and
    you react by?*
a. Thinking Hallowe'en isn't even over yet.
b. Start making a list of how many people
    you will need to buy gifts for.
c. Dread the thought of having to pay for gifts.

9. *You get an offer from your bank/broker offering you a free
    financial review. Do you?*
a. Make it your business to meet them
    and see what they have to say.
b. Delay the meeting for a year as such a review was
    carried out for you only twelve months previously.
c. Ignore the invitation. You don't need anyone
    else to tell you that the news is not good.

10. *How often do you check your current account for trans-
    actions/balances?*
a. Most days on-line.
b. Once a week.
c. Twice a month.

11. *You see a newspaper advert from a bank offering very low
    rates of interest for people switching mortgage to them. Do
    you?*
a. Enquire and see how much in total
    you could save by switching.
b. It reminds you to check and see what rate you
    currently have but you take no immediate action.
c. Switching? Couldn't put up with filling out
    forms again and having to pay legal fees.

12. *Do you know how much you are paying for life assurance/
    mortgage protection?*
a. Yes and I can tell you the life company if you want.

b. Yes, give or take €10 or €20

c. Do I have mortgage protection?

13. *Do you know how long your employer will pay your salary should you be out of work due to an accident/illness?*

a. Absolutely.

b. You're told three months but you have nothing in writing.

c. You're afraid to ask.

14. *You're planning a holiday abroad this year. Do you?*

a. Plan well in advance, knowing that you are going to pay for it from your holiday account.

b. Use existing savings to book and think about spending money nearer the time.

c. Get a top-up loan from your credit union because you are so stressed out from money worries that you need a holiday.

15. *Do you know how much you spent last month on take-aways and eating out?*

a. Down to an exact cent.

b. On average, yes.

c. Not really. Twice a week, I think, at €25 a time. What's with all the questions? I have to eat.

16. *You're doing your weekly shopping and are standing in line at the check-out when you notice that if you had the store credit card you would get a €40 voucher as a reward. Do you?*

a. Ignore the offer.

b. Take the leaflet to read later.

c. Sign up there and then.

17. *Do you ever check to see if you are entitled to claim any tax back for things such as medical expenses, college fees or service charges?*
a. Yes, I always make a quick phone call if I am in doubt.
b. Sometimes I do if I am reminded or
    it is brought to my attention.
c. Sure you can't claim for anything like that, I know
    that for a fact. Tax relief for my wheelie bin? Don't
    be ridiculous. I wouldn't waste my time checking.

18. *How often do you and your partner argue about money?*
a. Rarely.
b. Sometimes.
c. Often.

19. *You buy a very expensive item. How does that make you feel?*
a. Delighted. You saved long and hard for it
    and you appreciate it very much.
b. A little guilty but, hey, you deserve it.
c. The high soon wears off when you look at the receipt
    again and you try to convince myself it was a bargain

20. *How many credit cards do you have?*
a. One.
b. Two, Visa and MasterCard.
c. Two or more.

21. *You buy a scratch card and you instantly win €25,000. Do you?*
a. Spend some of it and put the rest into investments.
b. Pay off the credit cards and treat
    yourself to something luxurious.
c. Spend the lot! What are the chances of
    you winning that amount again?

22. *Your phone bill arrives and it is a lot more than you wish to spend. What do you do?*
a.   Look at alternative providers in the market, research call charges and line rental and find a cheaper plan.
b.   Put a 'check other providers' on a to-do list and place it on your fridge.
c.   Promise yourself you will cut down on calls but never bother.

23. *Which of the below do you think best describes your attitude to money?*
a.   Knowing you have savings gives you a great sense of security. You also want to get value for the money you earn.
b.   I save when I can. I know it is important but am not sure what is most important for me right now.
c.   I am no Shylock. Money is for spending.

How Did You Do?

Mostly A

You have your finances well under control and have a great attitude to how you spend your money. Your are willing to invest time and effort to find ways to maximise the return on your savings while looking for ways to minimise your outgoings.

You are not a penny-pincher but if you see an opportunity to pay less than what you are currently paying, you first familiarise yourself with the alternative, then make an informed decision.

You are ideally placed to begin paying your mortgage off or retire early because you have surplus income as a result of cost-saving measures.

Your are not concerned about being loyal to your bank, phone company or credit card provider, and feel that because it is your hard-earned money you want it to be used to its maximum potential for you and your family.

You should also bear in mind long-term financial planning considerations and should not try to do everything by yourself. Seek independent advice when it comes to planning for the future or when considering investing or borrowing money.

You do not have to be earning vast amounts of money to be an A-type person. This type of individual is just more cautious about what they spend their money on. Whatever their income level is they demand value for money.

MOSTLY B

You care about how much you are spending but you don't want a budget to rule your life.

You don't see the benefit of saving €50 or €100 here and there as it does not merit the effort you have to put in but you do go through phases where you are very aware of the products that are available that may be of benefit to you.

You suffer from the 'I'll call them or do that tomorrow' syndrome and rarely follow it through.

You are loyal and maybe too trusting of your bank and utility providers but with the right guidance and discipline you could improve your cashflow significantly without altering your lifestyle too much.

Remember to keep an eye on your finances a bit more and plan well in advance. You may need to set up two accounts: one for your holiday fund and another for bills, in which you lodge a portion of your income every month, rather than operating from just the one account.

Get a financial review done straight away and ensure that you have sufficient life cover in place for your spouse and children in the event of your death. Make sure you know how much – if any – of your income is protected by your employer should you be unable to work for a period of time.

MOSTLY C

You have no handle on your loan commitments, how much you are spending or what you are spending your money on. You are oblivious of the fact that you are throwing your money away; instead you complain that the cost of living is to blame. You are in denial about your mounting debt and believe it will somehow sort itself out. It is likely that in the future money issues could lead to conflict between you and your partner if they are not sorted out now.

You may have missed some loan repayments already and if you haven't you will – that is, if you don't get a grip on your finances quickly. You are likely to take on new debt thinking it will get rid of old debt and you may start hiding bills from yourself.

It doesn't matter whether we are A, B or C; we all need to start looking more closely at our finances and start 'micro-managing' how we spend our earned cash. If we do this we will improve our quality of life and our disposable income.

Let's start looking now at what we spend our money on. Get out a blank piece of paper because you will need it for the next chapter, and be prepared for a surprise.

3

Getting to Grips and Taking Control

Before you can decide on a particular course of action you have to know what you are up against.

Step 1

List all your debts, how much is owing, how much you pay each month, the organisation you owe it to, what interest rate you are being charged for each debt and how many years remain before the loan is cleared off in full. Now you know how much is outstanding altogether and how much of your income is going towards servicing these debts. You are going to be surprised and probably shocked at the combined total.

Let me give you an example of what you may be looking at:

Lender	Purpose	Amount Outstanding	Monthly Repayment	Term Remaining
Credit Union	Holiday	€7,200	€120	5 years
Credit Card	Visa	€10,000	€308	Open-ended
Bank	Car Loan	€23,500	€651	3 years
Bank	Personal Loan	€3,400	€156	2 years
Bank	Mortgage	€220,000	€1,051	35 years

You can see from the above that almost €2,300 each month is going towards servicing your short- and long-term debt. Therefore, this amount of money is not yours to spend when you get paid each month.

Over 50% of your fixed monthly outgoings may be going towards servicing your short-term debt and it is this amount that is putting people under pressure each month.

STEP 2

Now let's look at your other monthly outgoings. I want you to write down the amount you spend on the following:

Expense	Monthly Outgoing
Home insurance	
Mortgage protection/Life assurance	
Health insurance	
Gas/Electricity	
Phone bill	
Food shopping	
Eating out/take-aways	
Coffee/sandwiches	
Lunches	
Drinking out	
Smoking	
Petrol	
Car insurance	
Parking	
Satellite TV	
Club dues	
Clothing	
School expenses	
Pension contributions	
Pocket money	
Savings	
DVD/Video rental	
Regular charity donations	
Newspapers/magazines	
Mobile phone	
Total	

Many of you are now wondering exactly how much you do spend on each of the above.

If you don't know this off the top of your head look at your bank statements over the past three months. This should help identify how much you are spending in each category. This is a great exercise as it will highlight areas that you are spending a fortune on when you thought it wasn't so money-intensive: for example, take-aways, sandwiches and coffee at lunchtime, that cappuccino each morning. I don't want to sound like a Scrooge but cutting back just a little will help your cashflow enormously. For example, don't be afraid to bring your own sandwiches to work; if you do you could save yourself about €100 each month.

STEP 3

The third thing you do is write down what your total net monthly income is.

Source	Net Monthly Income
Earnings from employment	
Benefits including children's allowance, disability benefit, pension payouts etc.	
Income each month from savings/ investments you may have	
Rental income from an investment property you may own	
Other	
Total	

If your total income is less than your total outgoings you have a problem.

You may have too many loans or you are spending too much each month and not managing your finances properly – or possibly a combination of the two.

TAKE ACTION

You are now going to decide how to take action and tackle this debt.

Your existing debt may not even be the problem. It may just be that you are not managing your income properly each month, or spending too much on luxury items. Now I want you to write down your debt again, starting off this time with the debt that has the highest interest rate, then the next highest, and so on.

Your plan of attack is to start tackling the debt with the highest interest rate first and not the highest amount outstanding. This loan that is costing you the most each month, excluding your mortgage, is the loan you need to get rid of most quickly.

Let's look at your debt again but this time in order of the highest rate of interest.

Lender	Interest Rate	Amount Outstanding	Monthly Repayment	Term Remaining
Credit Card	18%	€10,000	€308	Open ended
Bank	15%	€3,400	€156	2 years
Credit Union	11%	€7,200	€120	5 years
Bank	9%	€23,500	€651	5 years

So any extra money that you can gain from cutting back on expenditure should be added to your monthly repayment in order to eliminate that high interest-rate debt first. For example, if you save €20 each month by switching to a new home-insurance provider this amount should go as an extra payment against your credit card balance or the personal loan that is being charged at 15%.

The next thing you should do is to start comparing your

existing loans with what other providers are offering. Why pay 18% interest on a credit card when other financial institutions offer 0% on balance transfers for six months, and maybe 9% thereafter. If you switch providers your full monthly repayment will go to reduce the capital outstanding and not just service the minimum repayment due.

How competitive is your car loan? Can you get a better deal from another lender? Every saving, no matter how small, will help your situation.

Don't forget your mortgage. There is much competition in the marketplace at present and banks are seeking to attract borrowers with lower rates than their current provider may be charging. Some lending institutions will pay all or part of your legal fees so there may be little or no cost for switching. Let me give you a quick example of this: a simple reduction of 0.3% on a mortgage of €400,000 would result in total interest savings of more than €24,000 over the life of the loan, with a reduction in monthly repayments of nearly €70.

HOW ARE YOU GOING TO DEAL WITH THIS DEBT?

The money is going to come from four places:

- Surplus income
- Savings made by adjusting your spending
- Existing savings
- Consolidating all your debt by remortgaging

SURPLUS INCOME

You can increase your surplus income in a number of ways. Getting a second job is an obvious one, suspending pension contributions for a period of time is another. If the opportunity exists, work overtime or an extra shift at least once or twice a month. But you can also increase your surplus income simply by altering the way you manage your outgoings each month. This may mean that you will have to make some tough decisions. You will reap the benefits of these decisions not just in the long term but very quickly.

SAVINGS MADE BY ADJUSTING YOUR SPENDING

Look for alternatives for buying your groceries. Are there cheaper outlets that sell exactly the same basic foodstuffs and household items but at a much lower price? You don't know? Well find out. Stop paying for things each month that you never use. Make a phone call to see if you can get cheaper car insurance or home insurance. Cost-saving measures such as these will leave you with more money each month that can be used towards clearing your debts much more quickly than you had thought possible. You will also be able to build up your savings.

It is very much a personal decision for you: is your priority becoming debt-free as fast as possible, or continuing to spend your money on items that support your current lifestyle?

Let's assume that you normally have two take-away meals each week at a cost of €50. If you cut back to just one take-away, and for one week each month bring your own lunch to work, this will save you about €150 each month or €1,800 per year! Can you believe that? These two simple changes could result in a personal loan being taken care of or part of your holiday paid for or a Christmas without stress. And with no major lifestyle change to boot!

What about checking to see if your home insurance is competitive? Find out how much you are paying each month and if you can get a better deal? Get a quote and see what savings can be achieved. Even if you only save yourself €20 per month it will be worth it. A saving of €20 per month could be put towards protecting your income against accident or illness or increasing your life assurance to ensure that your family is protected in the event of your death. You can now redirect the savings, however small, to other areas that are of importance to you. Do not dismiss the possibility of saving money, however small the amount is: remember it is your money!

Does it not bother you when you get your monthly statement from your bank and see charges applied to your account for direct debits and standing orders? It certainly bothers me. Many banks now offer free banking so why not make the switch and save on bank charges? Don't adopt the attitude that you are saving yourself only €150 per year and that it is not worth switching over for that amount. Remember it is the sum total of those savings that will make the difference to you. By the way, did you realise that if you saved €150 in bank charges each year, and applied this saving as an overpayment against your mortgage, you would reduce the term on a €200,000 mortgage over twenty years by nearly six months, saving yourself more than €4,300 in interest?

Finally, for those smokers reading the book: you know smoking is bad for your health and you know how much you are spending each day on cigarettes. Focus your mind on this figure: if you were to give up that twenty-a-day habit you would save more than €2,500 each year. But maybe you know that already.

EXISTING SAVINGS

If you have €10,000 on deposit earning 4% interest and €10,000 owing on your credit card which is being charged at 18% you may need to use your savings to clear your credit card debt immediately. However, if at all possible, try to leave money in your 'emergency fund' account. As a general rule don't exhaust all your savings if you can help it at all. If you can clear your debt from existing savings and still have surplus funds, fine, but if this is not the case, clear some of your debt and hold on to some savings for that rainy day, if it ever happens. The higher the interest rate on your borrowings the more important it is to clear as much as possible of them.

To help build up this emergency fund start by saving something right away. It does not have to be a big amount; just get into the habit of saving regularly. Treat saving money as a bill and tell yourself that it has to be done. Set up a standing order from your current account or better still ask you employer if they can deduct a certain amount from your salary each month and lodge it into a savings account.

I cannot stress this enough or say it too often: simply changing the way you spend your money, changing your attitude towards money and knowing what you are spending your money on will free up your cash to build this emergency fund.

CONSOLIDATING DEBT

If you have a property and you have sufficient equity in your home you could consolidate all your debts into one loan, secured on your house. This means rolling all your loans into one. The advantage of this is that your expensive loans are now absorbed into just one much cheaper loan, and repayments can be spaced out over a longer period of time, thereby reducing your monthly outgoings significantly.

Take the example of debts and loans outlined in previous pages. If you were to roll all the debt into one loan by remortgaging, the following would happen:

PRE-CONSOLIDATION

Lender	Purpose	Amount Outstanding	Monthly Repayment	Term Remaining
Credit Union	Holiday	€7,200	€120	5 years
Credit Card	Visa	€10,000	€308	Open ended
Bank	Car Loan	€23,500	€651	3 years
Bank	Furniture Loan	€3,400	€156	2 years
Bank	Mortgage	€220,000	€1,051	35 years
Total		€264,100	€2,286	

POST-CONSOLIDATION

Lender	Purpose	Amount Outstanding	Monthly Repayment	Term Remaining
Bank	Mortgage	€264,100	€1,264	35 years

By consolidation you will improve your cashflow by more than €1,022 each month, which is a considerable amount. The downside is that you will be spreading the cost of your short-term debt over a longer term so the amount of interest you repay will be more, a whole lot more. But if it means achieving a better quality of life for you and your family then so be it, as long as you are aware of what you are taking on.

Remember also that you are turning unsecured debt into secured debt by using your home as security, and if you fail to keep up your repayments on secured debt you could lose your home. You purchased too many items on that credit card and there is not a whole lot Visa can do about it but once you tie your house to that debt, you are placing it at risk should you not be able to meet your mortgage commitments.

I remember reading somewhere that consolidating debt is like sorting out your dirty laundry: you are not improving the situation, just moving things from one pile to another. In general you should try to avoid using an appreciating asset (your home) to fund depreciating assets – those items you bought with your credit card which may now be worthless.

If the reason you got into this mess in the first place was poor money management and overspending, consolidating your debt into one loan is not going to solve the real problem. You will improve your cashflow in the short term but are you going to slip back into the same bad habits? Are you going to rip up those credit cards or start using them again? You are surely going to change your car in another couple of years: how will you finance this new purchase?

When it comes to consolidation do not be seduced by advertisements which offer you the opportunity to save thousands of euro, and cash back, into the bargain. Look carefully at what the total life cost of the consolidation loan will be – not just your reduced monthly repayment.

If you are going to consolidate and save €1,000 per month on repayments, or whatever the amount may be, make sure you put the saving to good use. Don't just spend it without thinking first: set up that pension you could previously not afford; start a regular savings account; build up your emergency fund; allocate money to your children's educational plan; have a financial review carried out and make sure that you are adequately protected for life assurance and income protection.

If your handle it properly, consolidating all your loans into one lower-rate loan could be the solution for you. It could help get you out of that never-ending cycle of debt. But a word of caution – handled wrongly, it will just dig you into a bigger loan that ever and not improve your long-term situation at all.

To summarise, remember that before you can tackle your debt you need to know the following:

* Your total net monthly income
* Your fixed loan commitments
* How much you spend each month on variable items

You need to analyse what you are spending your money on each month. There are savings to be made if you want them: it just takes a little time on your part and less effort than you think.

Keep a record of how much you are spending each month and on what. After a month or so you will see how much of your money is being wasted. Set yourself a target of reducing your spend in each of the wasteful areas that you can identify. Look at alternatives, compare prices, do your research, It will be worth it, I assure you.

4

BUDGET AND PLAN

Anyone who has ever got into debt or has seen it increase to uncomfortable levels will at one time or other have vowed to change their ways and promised themselves that it will not happen again. So how do we keep an eye on our outgoings, hold on to more of what we earn and get us to that situation where we are financially sound? Where do we start?

I believe the answer lies with budgeting and planning.

BUDGETING

We hear the government say that each of its departments is allocated a certain amount of money annually to spend on their particular area, be that education, health or transport. The government knows exactly how much it can give and each department knows it can only spend the amount of money it receives.

That in essence is what a budget is: money coming in and money being allocated for different purposes. A projected budget is the expectation of future ins and outs. If we apply this principle to our income and household expenditure we should never have a need to get into that short-term debt such as borrowing for holidays, car insurance or Christmas expenditure.

Let's assume you take on the role of government in your house. Before you can give money out you first have to know what income you have. If you took the steps advised in the previous chapter you should know exactly the total net income you have to spend each month. If we continue with the government analogy we could refer to your fixed monthly outgoings as social welfare payments that have to be made by you, the government. Before any other money is allocated a certain proportion of your income has to be paid out to service your mortgage and other loans.

After paying this fixed amount your remaining income has to be divided between:

* The Department of Food
* The Department of Insurance
* The Department of Entertainment
* The Department of School
* The Department of Savings/Investments

Before you can give money out to these departments they (in other words, you) must first estimate what they will need to spend for the forthcoming month or year. You will then allocate your remaining funds in order of priority to each of the various departments. If one department has spent too much in the past (for example entertainment or eating out), it is small wonder if the minister was never told exactly how much he could spend. Similarly the Department of Savings may have had a raw deal and been given a very small share of the cake.

This is a light-hearted way of making a serious point: if you apply the same principles to your own finances that the government applies when drawing up its budget, you will get your debt and spending in order.

After a period of two to three months of recording what you spend your money on, you will be able to estimate accurately what your yearly spend in each area might be. You may then decide that more needs to be apportioned to savings and less to entertainment. You may realise that cost-cutting exercises need to be undertaken in areas such as food, insurance, transport – or whatever other area you deem appropriate.

At the beginning of each month you will have an allocation for food, transport, lunches, coffees and you will know not to spend more than that allocation in any given month. If you watch how much you are spending, at the end of the month you will not be using anybody else's money to pay for goods or services.

When people think of budgeting the very word conjures up images of cashflow reports or of Ebenezer Scrooge, pencil stub in hand, writing figures in a big ledger. So they shy away from it. Your budget does not have to be complicated, nor should you view it as being misery. It is just simple, prudent, thoughtful planning on your part and you will use it to keep on top of what comes in and what goes out each month.

You can write a budget out on a sheet of paper or use a straightforward spreadsheet document on your computer. Your budget may look something like thise:

Pay period ending (mm/dd)	Week 1	Week 2	Week 3	Week 4	Week 5
Income					
Take- home pay					
Fixed expenses					
Mortgage					
Car loan					
Credit union loan					
Personal loan					
Credit card					
Health insurance					
Home insurance					
Car insurance					
Variable expenses					
Gas/Electricity					
Food shopping					
Eating out/Take-aways					

Pay period ending (mm/dd)	Week 1	Week 2	Week 3	Week 4	Week 5
Coffee/sandwiches					
Lunches					
Drinking out					
Smoking					
Petrol					
Parking					
Satellite TV					
Club dues					
Clothing					
School expenses					
Pension					
Pocket money					
Savings					
DVD rental					
Charity					
Newspapers/Mags					
Mobile phone					

The above is just an example and the layout of the budget sheet can be altered to suit yourself.

After a while, budgeting will become second nature to you because your habits and attitude to money will have changed. You will know from keeping track of your budget what your household cashflow is and what you have to spend. If you monitor your budget correctly you won't have to worry about the dates in the month loans are debited from your account because if you don't go over your allocated budget you won't be overdrawn at the end of each month; it just can't happen.

The information that you record on your budget planner is pivotal to eliminating unwanted debt and to your ultimate financial success and I would stress that *you cannot reach your financial goals without it.*

If you have tried budgeting and don't understand why it is still not working, consider the psychological factors at work. Do you need to spend money on clothing, jewellery or cars to bolster your self-esteem? Is spending money becoming an addiction that you just can't stop? Do you see it as a sign of power? If you have answered yes to any of these questions you may need to seek professional help.

When drawing up a budget for the first time, or if you have tried and failed already and are going to give it another go – and I encourage you to do so – be positive about it. Consider it a spending plan rather than a cost-cutting exercise and before long you will see the beneficial impact of a budget on your finances.

If you spend less than you had budgeted by the end of a particular month, well done. You should do one of two things: either reward yourself by buying something nice or going for a nice meal out or else (the boring choice) put that surplus income into your savings account or use it as an extra payment for one of your high-interest loans.

PLANNING

Planning goes hand in hand with budgeting and it is defined as 'the psychological process of thinking about the activities required to create a desired future on some scale'. We plan for many things, such as:

- A deposit for a new house
- Retirement
- Holidays
- Christmas
- Weddings
- Starting a family

- Birthdays
- Redundancy

Let me take a deposit for a new house as an example of something for which you might plan. If you are thinking of purchasing a property, depending on your circumstances you may have to contribute 8% of the purchase price from your own resources before you can sign the contracts. You know this in advance. So what do you do? You start saving, of course, because you know that in six or twelve months' time you will have to have a certain amount of money if you want to fulfil your goal i.e. purchase your own home. You decide that you can afford to put away x amount each week/month and within a certain period you will have accumulated the desired amount. What you are doing is simply planning well in advance for that expected outgoing.

How do we plan for redundancy? What would happen if you were told by your employer that the business was closing down? Would you have sufficient resources at your disposal to pay your mortgage/rent and put food on the table for a few months until you find a new job. Or would you have to get a loan from your bank or a relative or start using your credit card. These things can be avoided if you plan for the eventuality.

Can you afford to have children? It is not strictly a financial decision but nowadays this is a question many couples are faced with asking themselves. An addition to the family brings many extra cares, including financial stresses – childcare, Bratz dolls – trust me, I know all about dolls from my two girls. These potential stresses can be greatly reduced by planning well in advance and knowing what to expect from the financial point of view.

What do planners do in their everyday job? Regardless of the industry in which they work they are engaged in forecasting that a particular raw material or computer part will be required on a particular date to allow production to continue without inter-ruption. From previous experience they know with a fair degree of certainty how much is needed, when it is needed and who needs it.

We should apply the same kind of planning techniques to our own personal finances.

We can predict with a fair degree of confidence (always allowing for price increases, which are well advertised) how much our telephone bill is likely to be every two months, what our gas bill will be, how much it will cost to tax the car, when our TV licence is due and what it will cost. We know that Christmas Day falls on 25 December and we know the date our children get summer holidays and the family holiday begins. With that knowledge we should plan that part of our salary each month is debited into a bills account, a Christmas account or a holiday account so that when those bills arrive every two months we are not wondering how we are going to pay them or having to take a big chunk out of our budget for other items. Why not set up a bills account or a Christmas and holiday account? Why must everything be debited from the one account? It doesn't have to be.

Let's look at an example. You know that your telephone bill averages €200 every two months. It's January and you have just paid it and it is not due again until March. For the next eight weeks why don't you lodge €25 per week into your bills account in anticipation of this bill. Part of your budgeting each week can be labelled 'future bills'. This is how you begin to micro-manage your money. Remember that planning for an expected bill is smart planning.

What do we do when we start a Christmas club? We are saving well in advance for that time of year where we know we will spend a lot of money on gifts and entertainment, but rather than borrowing for it or spending our Christmas bonus, we are planning months in advance to use neither. Instead we will use the savings that we have built up over the previous few months. Now that's good planning!

You probably have a calendar in your kitchen with all your family's birthdays, anniversaries, holidays. You keep this up to date to remind you of important forthcoming events. Why don't you get a second calendar and highlight on it the months you have to pay regular bills such as electricity and telephone or annual outgoings such as refuse bin collection, car tax and television licence? This system will highlight the months that require most financial outlay and will be a constant reminder to you of what has to be paid. This way you won't have any nasty surprises. After a while you will come to know what bills you expect without consulting your calendar and when that happens it is time to take it down.

5

CREDIT CARDS

What did we do before credit cards were so widely available? It may now seem hard to imagine how we would get by without them, but the reality is that it is becoming more and more expensive to live with them. The Central Bank announced, for example, that new credit card spending in Ireland in December 2006 was €1.2 Billion, up nearly 16% from the same period the previous year.

Credit cards come in a variety of different guises: standard card, gold card, platinum card, store card, with MasterCard and Visa in particular being the most widely used cards. The banks brand their own cards but MasterCard and Visa are the card transaction companies and they do the processing when you pay for things and then send the details back to the card providers.

The rate of interest, range of benefits and various gimmicks are used by the various credit card providers to sell us their card. Many of us use the credit card offered to us by our own bank and are largely unaware what interest rate we are being charged for purchases or cash withdrawals and what the late payment fees or over-the-limit fees are! For instance, do you know what rate of interest is being charged against your account?

There are many different factors to take into account when you are trying to decide which credit card is the best, but I feel the most important thing to know is not which card provider has the most to offer but rather what type of credit card user you are.

HOW CREDIT CARD PROVIDERS MAKE THEIR MONEY

Credit card providers make money primarily through interest charged on the balance outstanding on the credit card. This is supplemented in an enormous way by late payment fees applied to your account, over-the-limit fees and so on.

Credit card providers also offer payment protection insurance in the event of accident, illness or redundancy. Whilst this type of insurance can be worthwhile, it is an expensive protection for you to have and a very profitable one for the card company. It typically costs just under €1 for every €100 outstanding on your bill.

Card protection is another money-spinner for the credit card provider. If you lose your credit card or it is stolen, make one call and it will be cancelled, with a replacement card ordered. This is obviously worthwhile to have if for nothing more than peace of mind. The cost of this type of cover varies depending on how long a period you want cover for and it is normally within a range of €25 to €55 for cover of between one and three years.

TYPES OF CARDS

STANDARD CREDIT CARDS/GOLD CARDS

With a standard or ordinary credit card the provider bills the customer for purchases every month and you have approximately twenty-three days to pay. If your balance is paid in full during that timeframe then happy days – no interest charges accrue. However, if the full account is not paid then the rate of interest charged can be as much as 17%. If you use your card for a cash withdrawal, interest can be applied to your account from the date of withdrawal with a withdrawal fee to boot so it can be a very expensive way of getting access to cash.

Credit card providers have in recent years used a variety of clever marketing ploys, introducing gold cards, platinum cards and zinc cards to a wide number of people. In the past, cards of this type were apparently only offered to those who were rich enough to afford them and they were certainly a status symbol for their owners. Now credit card providers play on this status image and offer these cards to those who are not rich but have a certain level of income, not necessarily particularly high. The attraction of a gold card is hard to resist because some people are proud to be able to flash them around.

Cards of this type do not, however, necessarily mean that your credit limit is going to be any higher than with a standard card and such a card could also attract an annual fee along with the government stamp duty of €40!

STORE CARDS

Many retail outlets are now offering their own store credit cards which are operated for them by a financial institution. They are similar to ordinary credit cards in that interest is charged each month on the balance outstanding. They can be useful and convenient particularly if you shop quite a bit with one particular store or its affiliated stores. They encourage you to shop in one particular store and may offer you incentives such as discounts on items if your credit card is used to buy that particular item. This is fine if you pay the full balance owing but is not such a discount or 'bargain' if you do not manage to pay for it on time.

Apart from being offered discounts or being rewarded with bonus points on your weekly shopping you will achieve no real benefit from a store card, and your existing MasterCard or Visa credit card should suffice.

CHARGE CARDS

The most recognisable forms of charge card are American Express and Diners Club. They seem to be used by people who travel quite a bit or use their cards for large expensive purchases. They tend not to be as widely accepted in retail outlets as Visa or MasterCard but they are accepted in outlets where their users like to shop.

Charge cards may offer free travel insurance should you

book your holiday on-line – something that is not widely known by its cardholders. (More and more card providers are in any case offering this service to their members regardless of what type of card you have.) With charge cards you may have to pay an annual subscription – the amount depending on the card – along with the annual government stamp duty, so like the gold card they may not be cheap.

Charge cards have another advantage: it is possible to use them as a cheque guarantee card. You can get cash from your account without incurring any interest charges provided you have a credit balance there. For example if you have an American Express card you can cash personal cheques up to a maximum of €640 at any American Express office throughout the world.

THE ACTUAL COST OF MINIMUM PAYMENTS

The minimum payment is the amount you have to pay off your credit card balance before late payment fees are applied. The amount of this minimum payment is normally a certain percentage of the outstanding debt, typically between 2% and 3%, with a minimum payment of €10.

The danger of paying only a percentage of the outstanding debt is that as your debt gets smaller, so does the minimum amount you have to repay each month so your money is effectively being sucked into a compound interest sinkhole.

Let's look at an example of what I mean:

Let's assume the following:

Credit card balance	€5,000
Interest rate on your card	15%
Minimum pay calculated and paid (month 1)	€100

The minimum payment due for months 2, 3, 4 would reduce approximately as follows:

Month	Minimum Payment
1	€100
2	€99
3	€98

So it you were to repay just the minimum payment due each month on the above example it would take you thirty-two years, yes *32 years* to get rid of your debt by simply paying the minimum amount asked of you each month. In that time, by the way, you would pay €7,789 in interest.

As your minimum payment gets smaller the interest rate continues to compound, which is the credit card providers' perfect way to keep us in debt forever, with them reaping the profit.

So how do you solve the minimum payment problem? There is a simple way and it will make an incredible difference. Rather than continuing with the minimum the card company asks, you should continue with repayments of €100 per month, just as in the above example. If you look again at the example, you will see that it would take just *six-and-a-half years* to get rid of the same debt, paying €2,895.60 instead of €7,789.26 in interest.

It is worth comparing the two again:

Minimum payment each month	Thirty-two years to clear in full
Fixed repayment each month (minimum payment from first month)	Six-and-a-half years to clear in full

The difference in interest payments between the two is €4,893.

Simply by repaying the initial €100 every month the credit card holders eliminates this debt *twenty-six years* earlier and the interest cost is reduced by two-thirds.

BALANCE TRANSFERS

If you are committed to eliminating your debt and want to avoid paying exorbitant rates of interest on existing credit cards or store cards you should consider immediately transferring your card to a provider who is charging 0% on balance transfers.

Some credit card providers will offer 0% transfers for up to nine months for new cardholders. This means that everything you pay each month against the balance outstanding is repaying the debt and not covering any interest-rate charges. So, if you pay €200 each month for the next nine months your balance will have reduced by the full €1,800. By doing this you are obviously repaying your debt faster. If you are really serious about eliminating that debt altogether, when you get that new credit card from the company you just transferred to, take out a pair of scissors and cut the card in half. You don't need the card to repay the bills, the reference numbers will do. Getting rid of the card will remove that temptation to use it again.

If you decide to transfer your card to a special 'introductory' low-rate provider then be aware that this offer will come to an end at some stage, so find out what rate the card will revert to. Hopefully it will be less than what you were previously being charged. Why not check out whether other providers will offer you 0% interest on balance transfers at the end of your 'free period' and do the same with them? You could have a credit card for 12 months at 0% on balance transfers.

This switching will of course help greatly to reduce your debt but the secret to playing the credit card transfer game well is never to use the new card to buy anything. Remember the 0% interest is on transfers only and not on new purchases!

SAVINGS

I can't emphasise enough that if you have surplus savings that are earning little or no interest on deposit, you should withdraw them and use the money against your credit card bill. Nobody likes to withdraw all their savings, especially to repay a credit card debt,

but if you take care to lodge to a savings account the amount
you were paying against your credit card every month, you will
quickly build back the amount you used against your card.

CREDIT CARD HOUSEKEEPING

- Do not get into the habit of putting off
  your repayment past the due date.

- Set up a direct debit from your bank account that
  will allow the card provider to take the minimum
  amount due or the full payment from your account.
  Better still set up a standing order to avoid getting
  sucked into that minimum payment trap we covered
  earlier and pay the amount you decide is best.

- Only get a charge card if you know that you will
  pay the full amount due each month. Failure
  to do so will result in heavy penalties.

- Under no circumstances should you use your card for
  purchases when you have deliberately transferred your
  balance to new provider in order to avail of a low transfer
  rate. Again, the 0% interest offer applies to transfers only!

- Do not get a credit card because it 'looks nice'!

- Keep you PIN safe at all times.

- Keep a record of your monthly statements for reference.

- Check and see if there are other benefits attaching to the
  card, such as free travel insurance. In my own case, I found

this out only recently when my wife told me after she had
booked a holiday on-line for us and paid by credit card.

- Familiarise yourself with the rate of interest charged
  by your provider, their late payment fees, over-
  the-limit fees and cash withdrawal fees.

- Do not use your credit card for expensive purchases.
  Get a term loan from a bank or credit union; it
  may work out cheaper and quicker to repay.

- If you have cash in your wallet, use your cash
  to purchase. You may promise you will use that
  money to repay your credit card when you bill
  arrives the following month but you never do!

FINAL THOUGHT

Rip up your credit card if you are committed to eliminating the
money you owe on it. Set a fixed monthly amount that you are
committed to paying and are comfortable with. Work out how
long it will take to clear it and note the date in your diary. That
is the day you will be debt-free with your credit card. You will
remember this date as if it was a birthday!

6

GETTING THE BEST FROM YOUR MORTGAGE

There are more than two hundred different types of mortgage products available in the marketplace at the moment so it is essential that you are informed and receive good impartial independent advice, regardless of whether you are a first-time buyer, trading up, buying for investment or remortgaging. Some may be much more suitable than others to your present or future circumstances.

For example it is very important to research interest rates but it is also very important that when you compare rates you are comparing like with like. One lender may seem very competitive against another but are you comparing the same products? No two mortgages are the same. All lending institutions will advertise their most appealing offerings in order to entice new customers so be careful and be wary. Are they offering you introductory interest rates that last for twelve months and then increase dramatically in year two? Remember that for many of us a mortgage is a long-term commitment – a whole lot longer than one or two years – so what you want is to find at the outset the product and provider that are most suitable to you in the long run.

Some people tend to think that after a few telephone calls to different institutions to compare monthly repayments they have researched the market; they then choose the lender with the lowest monthly repayment. How many people opt for a one-year fixed rate just because the initial repayment is the lowest they find? Quite a few, to be honest, but the product with the most competitive rate is not necessarily the best mortgage for you. There is quite a number of other factors that should come into consideration when you are making your choice. While the interest rate may ultimately be the overriding factor in your decision, you should at least familiarise yourself with other aspects of your chosen product and lender, to ensure that you are not blindsided by some unexpected cost or restriction.

How many of you know what rate of interest you are currently being charged? How many of you know if you are on a fixed or variable rate mortgage? Not researching the mortgage market properly has led to people having very uncompetitive mortgages and paying way over the odds. Let's look at some of the various repayment options, products and providers available for you.

REPAYMENT OPTIONS AVAILABLE

As we all know, buying a home is one of the single biggest financial commitments most people will make in their lifetime. In most cases a mortgage is a long-term commitment and therefore selecting the right repayment type is crucial. This is generally the first step in your decision-making process.

There are typically two options that are available to you.

The first method is the *traditional annuity or repayment type mortgage*, in which your monthly repayment is made up of two parts, one that which goes towards the repayment of the capital sum borrowed and the second that goes towards repaying the interest charged on the amount you borrowed.

So, for example, should you borrow €400,000 over a thirty-year term at a variable rate of 4.60%, your monthly repayment would amount to €2,048 per month (excluding insurances and tax relief). This repayment is initially composed of €1,533 towards the interest repayment portion of the loan and €514 towards reducing the capital outstanding.

As can be seen from the breakdown of your monthly repayment, by far the greater part of your instalment in the early years will go towards repaying the interest portion of your loan and not until approximately year sixteen will more than 50% of your monthly repayment go towards reducing the capital you borrowed. The obvious advantage of this method of repayment is that you are guaranteed that at the end of the mortgage term your loan will have been reduced to zero with no further repayments needed. (This is, of course, assuming you stay in the same property for the term of your mortgage.)

Many of us may move house two, three even four times during our lifetime and it is reassuring to know that if we do move, whether it be after a year, five years or ten years each time we will have reduced the amount we originally borrowed under this method of repayment and each time we are increasing our equity – the amount we will take with us for our next purchase.

Above all, the interest and capital type repayment gives us peace of mind knowing we are reducing the amount we owe each month, and that the amount borrowed is guaranteed to be repaid in full over the term we choose.

The second method of repayment is an *interest-only method*, whereby the monthly repayment we make to our lender comprises interest only, and no part of the repayment goes towards reducing the amount borrowed.

For example, let's look again at borrowing €400,000 over a thirty-year term at a rate of 4.60%. The monthly repayment will amount to €1,533 but the loan amount will stay at the same level and you are not making any inroads into the capital borrowed.

The obvious major advantage of this choice of repayment is cashflow. On the sample mortgage you will save €514.67 per month by opting for the interest-only route. You may need this cashflow saving to repay a short-term loan or gift received from a parent or relative to enable you to put down a deposit on the property. However, there two very important factors to bear in mind before you choose an interest-only mortgage.

The first is to remember that during the entire term of the mortgage you will never reduce the amount you initially borrowed. You will have to bear in mind how you will eventually repay this amount. It may come from the sale of the property, an expected inheritance, a lump-sum benefit you are entitled to under your pension plan, or you just may not know at the time how you are going to repay. But you must be aware that it does eventually have be repaid.

The second factor I want you to bear in mind is that this method of repayment is available to you if you so wish. No two borrowers are the same – everyone has different requirements and needs – and we as advisers should not make up people's minds for them but rather listen to what they want and advise them about the options available that are most suited to their particular circumstances and best interests. I say this in light of a couple I know who told me that they were recently advised that they could not repay their mortgage in an interest-only way, a method that would have particularly suited them at that time.

If your disposable income position is tight and you are finding it hard to make ends meet, you may want the lowest gross outlay on your mortgage repayments in the short run. An interest-only option may allow you to put the savings in cashflow to better use, for example by repaying high-interest personal loans or credit card debt. After a period of years when your income has increased you could revert to an interest-and-capital-type repayment.

It is also worth remembering that by extending the term of your mortgage from the outset to thirty-five or even forty years you will keep your repayments at an absolute minimum and give yourself a margin of comfort should interest rates increase.

FLEXIBLE REPAYMENT OPTIONS AVAILABLE

Many lenders have now introduced a range of flexible repayment options that may suit the individual needs of some of their customers. These are a very welcome addition to the basic interest-and-capital and interest-only mortgage and can help greatly when you are planning your overall money-management strategy.

Some lenders are now actively marketing products such as a *deferred start* option which is specifically targeted at the first-time buyer. The idea behind this product is that your monthly mortgage repayments are deferred for a number of months, typically between three and six months, after your loan cheque has issued. The obvious advantage of this type of initial repayment option is that the borrower will benefit from not having any mortgage repayments at a time when cashflow may be extremely tight. They may set aside the monthly repayment they would normally have had to make so they can buy furniture for their new property, or repay some of a gift of money they got from their parents to enable them to buy the house. The downside of this choice is that the interest portion of the missed monthly repayment will be capitalised and your monthly repayment from then on will increase (this increase will depend on how many months you elect to miss) to ensure the your loan is repaid in full over the remaining term.

This type of product can be used to get you off to the right start. Many people save long and hard for their deposit and legal fees. but forget to budget for furnishing the property. I say 'forget' but I really mean 'postpone'. They know that money will be required to furnish the property and what do they do? They borrow the money or buy items with their credit card and this is typically how a cycle of debt begins. The deferred mortgage produce to which I am referring may give people the opportunity to put aside the amount they would have repaid on their mortgage for a number of months and use the funds towards the furnishings they require. My advice is to use your own savings rather than someone else's money!

Another product which is available from some lenders is often referred to as a *skipped month* option. This is geared towards existing customers. With this facility customers can opt to skip payments for one or two months during the year. This type of re-payment option is of particular use to people who would like to increase their cashflow at times of the year that are normally cash-draining such as summer holidays or Christmas. The repayments that are skipped are spread out over the remaining months of the year so that the term of the loan does not change. The negative feature of this product is the increased repayments during the remaining months of the year.

Using this type of product could be smart planning on your part. You might scarcely notice the extra amount you would need to pay throughout the year to make up for the two missed months and you might have no mortgage repayments in December or the month you are on holiday! Look at it as a form of Christmas or holiday club.

Other options available to existing borrowers including having a *mortgage break*. This option is available to clients who have a good track record with their current lender and who wish to suspend their monthly repayments for a period of time, perhaps because they have a baby or wish to travel or take a career break. At the end of the mortgage break the deferred repayments are added back on to the loan and your repayments will increase to ensure that your loan is repaid within the agreed term.

WHO WILL ARRANGE YOUR MORTGAGE?

Who arranged the mortgage on the property you currently reside in? Where do you go for a new mortgage or remortgage? Your can now arrange your mortgage from a variety of different sources. These are some of the factors that will influence your choice of provider:

- The amount they are willing to lend to you
- How competitive they are
- Customer service
- Flexibility (overpayments, underpayments, interest-only facilities, 100% mortgages, extended term, mortgage breaks)
- Fees, if any

* Reputation – do you know anyone who may
  have used the particular lender or broker before
  and how was their experience with them?

The following institutions all offer or arrange mortgages:

BANKS

The traditional high-street banks have years of lending experience
and are a major presence in towns and cities in Ireland. In recent
years they have become increasingly competitive and innovative
in the market, in response to new entrants in the Irish lending
market as well as the increased competitiveness of traditional
building societies. This has led to them to become more focused
on targeting new and existing mortgage business, and rates and
products they now offer are a testament to this.

The advantage of dealing with banks is being able to visit
them when you wish. If you have a problem or need to discuss a
particular aspect of your mortgage you can arrange a face-to-face
meeting with a member of staff.

You may be tempted to use your existing bank because it
is convenient for you and because they have all your details and
if anyone is going to give you money it is them. This could be a
mistake. What is a lender going to tell you? All about their own
products. They are hardly going to tell you that another lender
may be more suitable for you. Shop around; get the best deal
out there. Every lender has different criteria and each application
is judged on its own merits so one bank is not going to make it
easier or more difficult for you than another.

BUILDING SOCIETIES

In the past building societies were seen as the mortgage experts.
It was their main business – that and traditional savings accounts.
Their product-offering was traditionally very narrow but changes
in legislation allowed them to offer a wider selection of products
such as credits cards, car loans and life assurance products –

increasingly similar to the products offered by banks. However, their primary focus remains mortgage lending, whether it is to owner occupiers, investors, people trading up or those seeking finance to purchase a commercial property. Because they are mutual societies – owned by their members and run for the benefit of members rather than, for example, shareholders – their rates are very competitive.

SPECIALIST LENDING INSTITUTIONS

There are now some mortgage providers who will arrange finance for those who cannot, for whatever reason, obtain a conventional mortgage, for instance, people who have had arrears on mortgages or other loans in the past and have been refused by other mainstream lenders. You may not recognise the name of these lenders because they operate mainly via mortgage intermediaries. Make no mistake, you will pay a premium for a mortgage of this type.

Let me give you an example of the consequences of having an impaired repayment record by comparing the monthly repayments of a mortgage in the amount of €250,000 over a 25-year period with an 'impaired' lender and your normal mainstream lender:

Lender	Rate	Monthly Repayment
Normal Lender	4.6%	€1,402
Specialist Lender	7.6%	€1,860

You will agree that the difference in repayments – €457 per month – is massive, and depending on how bad your credit history is the rate charged could be even higher.

To repeat: *if you have a bad repayment history, you will pay the penalty.*

INSURANCE COMPANIES

Some insurance companies, traditionally seen as pension providers or life assurance specialists, have recognised an opportunity to offer mortgages to their new and existing customers. They can arrange your mortgage, your home and contents insurance, your mortgage protection requirements, all under the same roof, and this is one of the reasons they are now offering this additional mortgage service.

They are effectively acting as mortgage intermediaries but may be tied to one particular lending institution. The mortgage will be branded and advertised under the insurance company's name.

MORTGAGE BROKERS

The function of a mortgage broker is to source and arrange the available product that will best match their client's expectations and needs.

The broker's role should be to relieve the borrower of hassle and make a recommendation that is based on an independent assessment of the suitability of a particular mortgage. The broker will focus on the specific needs of the borrower to ensure that the lender and the product chosen are right for you. A good broker will go the extra distance to ensure you are well advised about what is and is not available to you and to secure the best possible deal on your behalf.

Dealing with brokers has obvious attractions: they have an intimate knowledge of all the lenders, their lending guidelines, their rates and their service. They obviously have a number of lending institutions to choose from should an applicant qualify for the loan amount requested. The broker will liaise with your solicitor, the bank, the builder and of course keep you in the loop to ensure that when a closing date is agreed with the vendor/ builder the funds will be with your solicitor. He or she will also deal with any hiccups that may have arisen in the interim.

Some brokers may be tied to certain lenders so you should

always ask your broker who they are authorised to deal with, if they going to charge any fees for arranging the mortgage for you and what their qualifications are. You will want to deal with a qualified, knowledgeable individual who is an expert in the mortgage area.

Do not choose a mortgage broker who is inextricably linked to an estate agent. Who is the broker really working for, you or the auctioneer? We have heard reports in recent months of mortgage advisers sharing information about you, the borrower, with their estate agent partners. The estate agent will then know the borrowing power of the client. Remember the higher the sale price on a property, the higher the commission the estate agents will receive.

Play it safe and smart: use a mortgage broker who is independent and has no connection with the estate agent through whom you are purchasing the property.

GETTING TO KNOW YOUR MORTGAGE PRODUCT

VARIABLE AND FIXED-RATE MORTGAGES

In the EU interest rates have increased by 1.5% in just over twelve months and if your mortgage is based on a variable interest rate you will have noticed a sizeable increase in your monthly repayments in this time. If, as predicted, rates increase further this year, you will continue to see increases in your monthly repayments.

Customers with variable rate mortgages will see their interest rate moving up or down in response to changes in interest rates worldwide or because of economic policy decisions taken by the European Central Bank. This means uncertainty for the customer and repayments can be difficult to budget for.

However standard variable rates are still appropriate for many borrowers. They do not tie the customer to a lender for any set period as the mortgage can be redeemed at any time without penalty. Up until the early 1990s the majority of mortgages in

Ireland were variable. The rate of interest charged to the account would change in accordance with the provisions of the contract whenever the market interest rate changed significantly enough for lenders to alter their pricing structures.

For other people a better solution is to choose a fixed-rate mortgage which protects them within the fixed rate chosen against further increases in interest rates. Fixed-rate mortgages are a straightforward, reliable product that everyone understands. The concept is simple: no matter what happens to base rates, your monthly repayments remain the same for the duration of the fixed period chosen. These mortgages are good for first-time buyers or anyone who is on a budget and needs the stability of a set monthly repayment. If interest rates go up, fixed-rate customers have the satisfaction of knowing that their repayments will not follow it. However, this also means that if they drop and stay low, your repayments will remain as high as ever for as long as the fixed period lasts.

Even if interest rates remain level, you are still likely to pay slightly over the odds because fixed rates tend to be offered at a higher initial rate than variable ones. This is considered a bearable premium for the peace of mind that a fixed rate gives you.

The price of a fixed-rate mortgage depends on the length of time you fix for: generally the longer you fix for, the higher the rate and consequently the higher your monthly repayments. You can fix from periods of one year right up to twenty years and rates vary from as little as 4.34% to 5.69% depending on the fixed term chosen.

It is very important not to fix for longer than you think will be useful for you, as one of the main disadvantages of fixed rates is that if you wanted either to remortgage or move to another property before the fixed rate term expires, you may have to pay a sizeable early redemption penalty for doing so.

Over the past ten years, fixed-rate contracts have become more popular. With such a contract you will effectively be taking a gamble on whether you will be better or worse off depending on how interest rates move in the marketplace during the fixed repayment period.

The choice of how long a fixed term you should take is a difficult one and there is no right or wrong answer. It depends on individual circumstances, how risk-averse you are and whether you can afford to make higher monthly repayments in return for the certainty of a fixed rate for say ten years, as against the lower payments on a one-year fixed rate. With rates still being relatively low, the temptation to fix for a long time is strong and people who have heavy financial commitments and look likely to remain on a tight budget for several years could benefit from fixing for a longer period of time. Long-term fixes are currently unpopular with both lenders and borrowers but they are a viable option if you decide you would benefit from that kind of security.

It makes sense to choose a fixed rate if you think that interest rates are likely to rise. Rates are still quite low, and while no one can be absolutely certain which way they will go comments made recently by leading economists suggest that the ECB may increase rates by a further 1% within the coming year. So now may be a good time to fix your mortgage.

What happens after your fixed rate expires? Your lender will normally write to you about a month before the expiry and outline the options available to you. So you will be given an option to choose a fixed rate for another year or longer, or perhaps revert to a variable-type repayment. When choosing your lender always ask whether the rate offered to you when you were a new customer will be the same when the fixed-rate period is up for renewal. Some lenders may distinguish between new and existing business and increase the rate for existing customers. The difference may be substantial.

In summary, fixing your mortgage rate protects against market volatility, giving peace of mind because repayments will not change during the fixed term. On the other hand you cannot avail of reducing variable rates should they happen, you are liable to penalties should you decide to sell your property, and your fixed rate mortgage is just not as flexible as a variable rate one when it comes to overpayments or capital reduction payments.

You can also split your mortgage, with half at a variable rate to facilitate overpayments and to allow you to benefit from interest-rate decreases. By fixing the other half you will be protected from further rate increases and your mortgage will be easier to budget for. By taking this route you will be hedging your bets and getting the best of both worlds but again, and I cannot stress this enough, the choice is very much a matter for each individual.

PROS AND CONS
- Variable-rate mortgages are not ideally suited to those on a budget.
- With a variable-rate mortgage you can redeem your loan in full or make large partial lodgements against the amount outstanding without incurring any penalties.
- Fixed rates may be higher than some variable offerings.
- Fixed rates are ideal for first-time buyers or those on a budget.
- High redemption penalties can apply should you break your fixed-rate agreement.
- Fixed rates are worth considering if you think rates are on the increase.
- Your monthly repayment will remain the same for the duration of the fixed rate chosen.

TRACKER MORTGAGES
Lenders have the right to change their standard variable rate regardless of changes to the European Central Bank base rate, although the majority of lenders broadly follow it. Tracker mortgages bypass this possibility by mirroring exactly any changes to the ECB base rate.

Interest rates on tracker mortgages are charged at a set percentage above the ECB base rate and will vary depending on (a) the amount you are borrowing against the value of the property you are offering as security (so typically the lower the risk to the mortgage provider the better the rate they are likely to offer) and (b) the amount you are borrowing. It may decrease above a certain threshold. The margin above the ECB base rate will remain constant for the duration of the mortgage or until you switch product or lender.

Tracker mortgages offer some security as the rate is guaranteed never to exceed the base rate by more than a fixed margin. Payments will fluctuate over time as the ECB's base rate increases or decreases so they may not be suited to those on a strict budget.

With a tracker mortgage, you will benefit instantly from any drop in interest rates, which means you will know immediately what your rate will be as soon as the ECB announces it, whereas if your mortgage is on a standard variable rate you may have to wait and see what the lender does in response, and even then you may not significantly benefit from any cuts passed on by the ECB.

With a tracker mortgage any fluctuation in rates will have an effect on your monthly repayment: a rise will increase your repayment and a decrease will obviously reduce your monthly repayment. This makes budgeting far more difficult and if you cannot afford for rates to increase by more than a certain percentage you may not want to take the risk with this type of product or indeed any type of variable-rate product.

The advantages of a tracker mortgage are that if you have a loan with a low loan to value ratio (that is, if your property is worth a great deal more than the amount you borrow), your interest rate could be as low as 4.02% compared to the lowest standard variable rate in the market which at the moment is about 4.60%. There will be a significant difference in repayments here. Also, you have a guarantee that your mortgage rate will always be within a certain margin of the ECB base rate.

The method of repayment of a tracker mortgage is exactly

the same as all other mortgages, in that you can make interest and capital repayments or indeed interest-only repayments. Additionally, you have the facility to make overpayments on a monthly basis or lump-sum repayments to the amount outstanding.

PROS AND CONS

- This product directly follows the changes in the base rate of the European Central Bank.
- The margin set above the base rate will depend on the amount you are borrowing and your loan to value ratio.
- You will benefit from decreases in your repayments with rate reductions but you are also exposed to the risk of your monthly repayments increasing should rates rise, so this product would not be suited to those who are working on a tight budget.
- You will always know what the margin charged above the base rate is so this is in some ways a fairer system than the means by which standard variable rates are determined.

OFFSET MORTGAGES

With an offset mortgage account, all your finances are interlinked so your mortgage, current account and any other savings account you have are with the same lender. Basically the accounts you hold in a credit manner – savings and current accounts – are offset against those that are in a debit situation – your mortgage account.

Let's assume you have a mortgage where the balance outstanding is €400,000 and the interest rate charged to this account is 4.6%. Your financial assets are a combination of your current account where your salary is lodged and a savings account (all with the same financial institution). Let us assume that you have €9,000 in the savings account and an average daily balance in your current account of €1,000 and remember your mortgage outstanding is €400,000.

With an offset mortgage, the lender will normally not pay interest on your €9,000 savings in the traditional way. Instead, rather than charge 4.6% on your €400,000 mortgage, they charge interest on the €400,000 minus the €9,000 in savings and the €1,000 in your current account. This will mean that they will charge interest on a total of €390,000 rather than €400,000.

This means that your €10,000 will, in essence, be accruing interest at 4.6%. If this 4.6% was paid to you in the normal way you would owe tax on the interest earned. To get this sort of return on a normal investment, you would have to earn around 6% gross interest (before tax), although the amount of tax paid would depend on your annual income.

By choosing this type of mortgage account and maintaining it in the correct manner you could save money in interest charges and repay your mortgage earlier than you anticipated.

PROS AND CONS

- Offset mortgages are suitable for people who are good at controlling and monitoring their finances on a monthly basis.
- You can still make over- and under-repayments to your mortgage account.
- They are ideal for those who have a mortgage and also have medium to large savings accounts that are earning very little deposit interest.
- You can repay your mortgage in a much shorter period of time if you operate the account in a proper manner but you have to be disciplined and committed to this course of action.

REMORTGAGING

The past number of years have seen a significant number of people remortgaging and I expect this trend to continue for the foreseeable future. People are concerned that, should interest rates continue to rise in the coming months, they will have problems servicing their mortgages along with other debts. People are also becoming increasingly aware of the benefits of remortgaging: they see it a way to help them manage all their finances.

It is amazing how little attention people pay to their mortgage once they have arranged it and it has taken effect. People complain when they see the rates on offer to new borrowers and feel aggrieved as an existing customer that the same rate is not offered to them. The solution to this frustration may lie with remortgaging.

WHY REMORTGAGE?

You could remortgage for a couple of reasons. The first reason is to switch from your current provider to another who is offering you a better interest rate. The rate reduction would have to justify the switch when legal fees, for example, are taken into account. However, it is common nowadays for lenders to offer to pay your legal fees if you switch your mortgage to them.

Let's look at examples of the rates that are applied by a number of different lenders and the corresponding monthly repayments. Let's assume a mortgage amount of €400,000 over a thirty-year period with repayments based upon a standard variable rate:

Lender	Rate (APR)	Monthly Repayment
Lender A	4.65%	€2,040
Lender B	4.69%	€2,052
Lender C	4.80%	€2,064
Lender D	4.90%	€2,088

Lender E	4.96%	€2,108
Lender F	5.00%	€2,112

When people do explore the idea of remortgaging solely in order to find a lower interest rate and discover that they will save only €40 each month they feel it is not worth the hassle. Certainly, the difference is not life-changing now but over a thirty-year period on a loan amount of €400,000 you would save nearly €19,000 or have your mortgage cleared off sixteen months earlier. Would you prefer to give your bank an extra €19,000? If so, fair enough – they will gladly accept it from you.

REPAY YOUR LOAN FASTER WITH YOUR LOWER RATE

If you move from one lender to another for a cheaper rate the trick is to continue with the same monthly repayment as before (for the higher-rate mortgage). This will reduce the term on your mortgage much more quickly and you will save thousands of euro in interest.

Let me give you an example of what this saving would mean, using the figures outlined above:

From lender	To lender	Monthly saving, used as overpayment	Mortgage term reduced by	Interest saving
B	A	€12	4 months	€4,982
C	A	€24	7 months	€9,807
D	A	€48	16 months	€19,018
E	A	€68	24 months	€26,279
F	A	€72	25 months	€27,689

When you see the above does it make you wonder how much you can save? Do you now think it worth the hassle of switching? I believe it is.

The number of people who are currently repaying at least 0.5% more than what they could be repaying is staggering. Whose fault is it? Their own. Let me ask you about rates but this time your own mortgage rate. What is it? Don't know? Well find out and find out fast.

DEBT CONSOLIDATION

The second and more popular reason for remortgaging is debt consolidation. That is the grouping together of all your loans into one loan with one monthly repayment. This can be done if you have sufficient equity in your property so that (a) there are funds available to clear off the remaining balances owed on your other loans and (b) there is sufficient comfort from a lender's point of view that you can repay this increased amount which, don't forget, will be secured on your private residence. Normally a lender will not advance more than 90% of the value of your property for remortgaging, with many only advancing up to 85%. So, assuming your house is valued at €200,000 you could remortgage up to a maximum of €180,000, that is 90% of €200,000. Let's look at the following example:

PRE-REMORTGAGE

Lender	Purpose	Amount Outstanding	Monthly Repayment
Credit Union	Holiday	€7,200	€120
Credit Card	Visa	€10,000	€308
Bank	Car Loan	€23,500	€651
Bank	Personal Loan	€3,400	€156
Bank	Mortgage	€220,000	€1,051
Total		€264,100	€2,286

POST-CONSOLIDATION

Lender	Purpose	Amount Outstanding	Monthly Repayment
Bank	Mortgage	€264,100	€1,264

The saving each month is €1,022.

When you are taking over short-term debt it is very important to be aware of the fact that you could be financing that car or personal loan over a much longer period that you had initially anticipated. Your total repayments are reduced because you are financing everything over a fifteen- or twenty-year term at home-loan rates. The advantage to structuring your debt this way is that you will improve your cashflow considerably.

When remortgaging you have an option to structure your loan in such a way so that the car loan you consolidated with your mortgage is still repaid over a three- or four- year period. The cash-flow savings will not be as great but it is an option available to you and one which you should explore. Compare the two options and decide which one suits your present circumstances best.

IS REMORTGAGING WORTH THE HASSLE?
When people think of remortgaging, it conjures up images of financial strife, but nothing could be further from the reality. Remortgaging can be a very positive experience. There can be some initial expenses but, as shown above, massive savings can be achieved.

Although the process of remortgaging is similar to getting a normal mortgage, it is faster because you are not buying a home. Depending on the lender, it should take around five to six weeks. If you need to remortgage fast, some lenders offer fast-track services the can complete in as little as ten days, but it does depend on your individual circumstances.

When deciding whether to remortgage or not, you need to think about what you get out of your current mortgage as well

as what you want from a new product. These are some of the
questions you should ask yourself:

- What are my current repayments and
  am I able to lower these?
- Can I get a better deal from my existing lender?
- Does my rate still meet my requirements,
  for example fixed or variable?
- What costs are involved?
- Am I saving enough to justify remortgaging?
- Does my existing mortgage have
  any redemption penalties?

How to Be Mortgage-Free in Ten Years

For many of us a mortgage remains a huge psychological barrier
standing firmly in the way of financial freedom. Being in debt forever has become a real possibility for homeowners, particularly
with spiralling house prices, higher than ever mortgage amounts
and interest-only loans. These factors have resulted in huge loans
that we grudgingly spend most of our adult lives repaying.

Unless we win the lottery repaying a mortgage of, say,
€200,000 in less than ten years will be beyond the means and
the willpower of most borrowers. You could work eight days a
week and live on baked beans until your loan is cleared but for
the majority of us this is unrealistic.

However, there are less drastic and even some obvious
measures that can make a big difference over time. These can
help eliminate your mortgage and other debt altogether within a
very short space of time, resulting in your being mortgage-free in
less than ten years.

For example if you have a mortgage of €200,000 and used
the maturity of your SSIA account, let's assume €20,000, as a
lump sum against your loan amount and continued with your
SSIA contribution – €254 per month – as an overpayment, you
would reduce the term of your mortgage from twenty years to

fourteen years ten months. An additional €100 overpayment would reduce your term to just thirteen years six months.

This reduction in term can be achieved by simple, common-sense planning and by restructuring your mortgage repayments. This is not rocket science, just careful planning. If you made no further repayments in the first example outlined above you would save yourself over €34,000 in interest alone.

That was to show you how to reduce a mortgage term by six-and-a-half years. How can you reduce it further still? Did you know that by cutting back on some luxury items you would pay your mortgage earlier and save the following interest against a twenty-year mortgage?

Digital TV subscription	nine months off your mortgage and €4,333 in interest savings
Ten cigarettes per day	two years two months off your mortgage and €11,691 in interest savings
One cappuccino per day	ten months off your mortgage and €4,583 in interest savings
One chocolate bar per day	six months off your mortgage and €2,805 in interest savings
One pint of beer per day	two years three months off your mortgage and €12,423 in interest savings

By cutting out these five everyday items you will reduce your mortgage by six years six months and save over €35,836 in interest.

Other means of reducing or eliminating your mortgage altogether:

- Stop pension contributions and use the funds towards overpaying your mortgage. Then restart contributions after you become debt-free.
- Explore ways to boost your income, for example by finding a second job. This will depend on how committed you are to the cause.

- Rent a room and earn up to €7,620 each year tax free.
- Make your own lunch.
- Pay off your credit card bill in full each month.
- Undertake home improvements to add value to your property. This will reduce the amount repayable when you sell your house.
- Manage your current outgoings. What are you spending your money on each month? Explore cheaper alternatives for health insurance, car insurance and home insurance.
- Structure your finances better and set a budget for how much you are going to spend each month. Your lifestyle does not have to change drastically but your quality of life will if you become mortgage free. Think of the things you could do with your surplus income.

By repaying your mortgage earlier you will save tens of thousands in interest payments. This could allow you to:

- Invest in a second home or investment property at home or abroad
- Take that dream holiday you always wanted
- Pay for your children's education without difficulty
- Plan for a retirement that you can now afford

'What can be added to the happiness of a man who is in health, out of debt, and has a clear conscience?' Adam Smith

I could not agree more.

Mortgage debt is our biggest debt and definitely the best debt we could have. Just make sure your existing provider is suiting your needs and is competitive. Research the market, compare lenders, don't discount small savings. As you can see from previous pages a small saving each month can lead to a much bigger saving in the long run. Explore the possibility of overpayments each month and perhaps think about transferring to an offset mortgage account. The savings you can achieve will stagger you. Consider putting your SSIA savings amount towards your mortgage and you could take years off the term.

By getting to grips with your mortgage you are going to be in a better position to make an informed decision as to whether your current provider is doing enough for you. If you don't have the time to do the research yourself then get an independent, qualified mortgage adviser to help you.

7

SAVE, SAVE, SAVE

'How can I save when I have no money?'
'I just can't get into the habit of saving.'

These are the excuses I hear every day from people for whom
I carry out financial reviews. I start to talk about savings and investments and ask them how much they have set aside and this is
what I am told. It surprises me at times when even people whom
I considered financially astute neglect the savings habit.

I believe that learning to save is having the right attitude.
Many people develop this attitude at a very early stage in life,
that is when their parents educate them on the value of money
and the importance of having a savings account. They find out
how gratifying and easy it is to save, and purchase something
with their own pocket money, and they realise how much more
they appreciate the item bought in this way. But anyone can
become a saver at any stage in their life.

WHY DO WE NEED SAVINGS?

The stark reality is that unless we have savings to fall back on in
times of illness, redundancy, accident or death we run the risk of
losing our home, running up a credit rating that could take years
to repair, borrowing from relatives or worse still, moneylenders.

Statistics show that at some stage in a person's life he or she
may suffer from a significant loss of income. This could be as a
result of:

- Unemployment
- Serious illness
- Death of an income-earning spouse
- Separation or divorce
- An accident which prevents you from working. (I refer specifically here to those who are self-employed.)

Some of you may have been asked to attend or contribute to a benefit night in aid of someone who may have broken his leg playing soccer, who was self-employed and had no income for three or four months? I know I have always thought this a terrible predicament to be in.

Other, less significant events may occur but having some savings will always help to soften the blow when:

- The car needs a major repair.
- A kitchen appliance needs to be replaced.
- It is the beginning of winter and you realise your oil tank is empty.

THE EMERGENCY FUND

You need to start saving now for an emergency fund that you can call upon in the event of an unforeseen occurrence. This fund is not a Christmas fund or a holiday fund; it does 'exactly what it says on the tin' and is called upon when needed. When the need arises you will simply use your savings rather than having to borrow money.

The amount of money you should aim for in this emergency fund is about three-to-four months after-tax income. This should give you a sufficient amount of money if you need to find a new job. There is no right or wrong amount and the sum of money required will depend on your own individual circumstances, but I suggest that you aim for a minimum of three times your net monthly income.

BUILDING YOUR FUND

Here are some suggestions for how you can start building your fund:

- Start saving today. It does not have to be a large sum to start with. Even on the tightest of budgets a small amount will add up over time.
- If you get a pay rise or an increase in your take-home pay because of a tax change in the budget, put half of this amount towards your savings account. You did without it before so you won't miss it now.
- Ask your employer if they can deduct a percentage of your salary each week or month and redirect this to a savings account for you. After a while you will become used to your new salary level.

If you were contributing to an SSIA account you will know how quickly a fund can grow over a relatively short space of time. It is not going to happen overnight either so don't worry if it takes two or three years to achieve. Start off slowly with a manageable amount, adopt a positive attitude and before long you will be there.

Once you have that money tucked away it will give you tremendous peace of mind.

A WORD TO THE SELF-EMPLOYED

It is very important that self-employed people save money for another very important reason, *their tax bill*. Rather than being faced with having to come up with a lump sum when returns are being made each year, it is prudent to set aside a certain amount of money each week or month.

Work with your accountant on this one. You know how much you have paid in previous years and you can estimate your likely income for the forthcoming year so direct a certain percentage each month into a separate savings account used only for the payment of taxes.

WHAT ARE YOU SAVING FOR?

I believe that having your emergency fund in place should be your number-one priority when it comes to savings. There are however many other reasons for saving money regularly which can be classified as short- and long-term goals.

You may, for example, want to accumulate a fund that will pay for your summer holiday, gifts at Christmas time, home improvements. These goals tend to be short term in nature and can be reached typically within six to eighteen months. The amount required will obviously dictate how long it will take you and how much you can comfortably set aside each month.

Longer-term goals may include a deposit for a new house or a second property, upgrading your car, a conservatory, educational fees, and these tend to take in excess of five years before the desired fund is attained.

It is very much down to the individual how committed and dedicated he or she is to reaching the goal. No matter how long it takes, the common denominator for everyone is that they are saving for a specific purpose – they have a particular use for their savings.

It may be easier for people to save when they have a short-term goal in mind – for instance a big-screen plasma television – and a tangible result after a relatively short period of time, than it is to create their emergency fund. The point of an emergency fund is that it is not spent, but put aside in case of illness or unemployment. It is, however, the most important form of savings you can make.

YOUR SAVINGS PLAN

I want you get out a pen and paper and start thinking about what you would like to save for in the short and long term. Put a price on each item. You could probably borrow for many of the things on your list but the purpose of saving is to get away from that all-too-easy route of borrowing for everything and racking up your personal debt.

Create a savings schedule that might look something like this:

Short-Term Savings, May 2007

Purpose	How much?	Needed when?	Amount required
Summer holiday	€3,000	18 months	€38 per week
Christmas	€1,500	12 months	€30 per week
New kitchen appliances	€700	10 months	€16 per week

You yourself will obviously determine the purpose and the amount required but a plan like this will help you focus your mind on having to set a certain amount aside if you want to achieve the desired goals. If there is just one goal, focus on that. You might find it useful to focus on items for which you have had to borrow money in the past.

Similarly, have a long-term savings schedule which may look like this:

Long-Term Savings, January 2007

Purpose	How much?	Needed when?	Amount required
Upgrade car	€10,000	5 years	€166 per month
College fees	€20,000	15 years	€111 per month
Anniversary cruise	€6,000	5 years	€100 per month

Saving for the above items obviously comes at a cost each month but if you have a structure, become disciplined in spending and focus on finding goods and services at more economical prices, you should have extra money to save. For example, if you find

cheaper home insurance and life assurance, thus saving yourself
€20 per week, you could add that amount to your summer holiday
saving fund.

SAVING TIPS

- Open a savings account separate to your current
  account. It can be with your local bank or credit union
  but its sole purpose is for savings. In this way you can
  see your savings grow. You will also be discouraged
  from withdrawing and spending the money!
- Ask your employer to divert a certain sum from
  your monthly salary to your savings account.
- Start off with an affordable amount each month. Be
  realistic as to how much you can comfortably set aside.
- Think of savings as if it were a bill. It
  has to be done and paid for!
- Use an old-fashioned money box and deposit
  your loose change in it every day.

GET YOUR CHILDREN SAVING

Start to get your children into the saving habit too. Talk to your
children about the value of money and the importance of saving
regularly. Get them to put aside some of their weekly pocket
money into their money box or into their own account. Reward
them with a bonus if they reach a certain amount; for example
when they reach €50 give them a €10 bonus.

If your children see a toy and you buy it immediately for
them they will have no concept of saving. Get them to do a
savings plan like you are going to do, and they will soon get
into the habit of saving first and buying that toy with their own
money.

They will begin to learn the value of money and appreciate
the toy all the better. It may take them three or four weeks to
save the amount they need but do you know what? They won't

mind and the excitement and anticipation builds as the target gets closer.

Let me give you an example of this. My daughter Rachel loves Bratz dolls and her room is full of them. It seems that each week a new one is for sale and they are certainly not cheap. Anyway a new 'Sheradon' doll was for sale at a cost of €30 and Rachel wanted to buy her. So what my wife Roseann did was to create a chart like this:

					Sheradon

Every time Rachel got her pocket money she placed it in her money box and ticked off a box which represented €1. If she got extra money from her grandparents or the tooth fairy she would deposit the amount in her money box too. After a short while the chart looked like this:

X	X	X	X	X	X
X	X	X	X	X	X
X	X	X	X		
					Sheradon

The chart was on the fridge and Rachel could see the empty boxes getting fewer and fewer as the days went by, until the day came when she had enough to go and buy the doll.

The importance of doing this kind of training is twofold. First you are getting your child into a savings routine and secondly you are not spending a fortune on toys, also saving money for yourself. This is not being mean; it is just commonsense money management.

SAVING TAX

Everybody can make some savings through the tax system. Do you know what you are entitled to? If so are you claiming your allowance? We all believe we are paying too much tax and because many of us are not claiming what we are entitled to, this is almost certainly the case.

Here are some of the allowances which may be relevant to your situation.

HEALTH EXPENSES

You are allowed to claim at your highest rate of tax for certain medical expenses incurred by you, your spouse, your child or a dependent relative.

The first €125 of your claim or €250 in respect of a family is not allowed.

You cannot claim for payments which will be reimbursed to you by a health-insurance provider, for example VHI, Vivas or Bupa, or by your local health authority.

If you have qualifying medical expenses amounting to €600 for you and your family and you are paying tax at the higher rate you are entitled to a tax rebate of €144. You can claim this relief by completing a Med 1 form.

Note that certain medical expenses such as dental treatment (except orthodontic treatment) and eye testing do not qualify for tax relief.

SERVICE CHARGES

Tax relief is allowed to those who pay local authority charges on domestic water supply, refuse collection or even sewage disposal. You are also entitled to tax relief on refuse collection where you use an independent contractor or for a group water scheme for domestic supply. Relief is given on charges paid for in the previous year and the maximum relief allowable from 2002 onwards is €400 per year at the standard rate of tax.

For example, if you paid service charges of €300 in 2006 you will be entitled to a tax credit of €60 (€300 x 20%) in the year 2007.

In order to claim for this a form IT27 will have to be completed.

MEDICAL INSURANCE PREMIUMS

Insurance premiums paid to authorised insurance providers are granted tax relief at source at the standard rate. You therefore pay a reduced premium of 80% of the gross amount due. There is no need to complete forms to claim this relief.

TAX RELIEF ON MORTGAGE INTEREST PAYMENTS

Relief is granted on moneys borrowed to purchase, improve or repair your principal private residence. This relief is granted on the interest element of your mortgage payment each month.

The maximum amount that can be claimed will depend on your status, for example:

Status	Single	Married	Widows/Widower
First-time buyer	€8,000	€16,000	€16,000
Non first-time buyer	€3,000	€6,000	€6,000

Relief is granted at the standard rate of tax and like medical insurance premiums is granted at source. If you are a first-time buyer make sure you complete a TRS1 form and if you change lenders you will need to complete this form again.

When you get an annual mortgage statement from your mortgage provider it should indicate the amount of tax relief given in that year. If you are making mortgage payments and think you are not receiving tax relief you should contact your local revenue office.

Trade Union Subscriptions
If you are a member of a trade union, your subscription entitles you to a tax credit of €60 at the standard rate of tax, currently 20%.

Permanent Health Insurance Premiums
Should you take out an insurance policy which protects and replaces your income in the event of your suffering an accident, illness or disability which prevents you from earning an income, you can claim tax relief on the premiums up to a maximum of 10% of your annual income.

Relief is granted at your marginal rate of tax. For example if you take out an income protection policy which would pay an annual benefit of €50,000 and which costs you €100 per month you can claim tax relief of 41% (€41) so the net cost to you each month is just €59.

Home Carer's Allowance
A tax credit of up to €770 is available should one spouse work at home caring for the couple's children, a person over sixty-five, or a person who is incapacitated.

Provided the home carer's income is not greater than €5,080, full relief is given; however, should the carer's income exceed this amount, a reduced tax credit will apply up to a maximum income of €6,620.

Rent a Room Relief
You are allowed to earn up to €7,620 each year in rental income without having to pay any tax where a room in your private/main residence is let as residential accommodation. Your mortgage interest relief is unaffected by this. Note, however, that you will

be taxed on the full amount of rental income should it exceed the threshold of €7,620 and not just the excess.

CHILDCARE SERVICE ALLOWANCE
You are exempt from income tax should you decide to provide childcare services for no more than three children in your own home, up to a maximum annual income of €15,000 in 2007.

RENT RELIEF
Tenants living in private rented accommodation can claim tax relief in respect of the rent they pay.

Relief is granted at 20% subject to the following maximum limits:

Single	Tax Year 2007
Under 55	€1,800
Over 55	€3,600
Married/Widowed	
Under 55	€3,600
Over 55	€7,200

In order to claim this relief a Rent 1 form needs to be completed.

TUITION FEES
Tax relief is available for certain full- and part-time postgraduate and undergraduate courses. This relief applies on fees up to a maximum of €5,000 per year. If you are paying fees for yourself, your spouse or child to a private or publicly funded third-level college you can claim relief.

The course must be an approved course in an approved college in the state or another EU member state. Claims for more than one child can be made and qualifying relief is given every academic year.

In order to qualify for this relief, note that undergraduate courses, be they full- or part-time, must be at least two years in duration and post-graduate courses not less than one year but not greater than four.

PENSION CONTRIBUTIONS

If you are a member of your employer's pension scheme, you can get relief at your highest rate of tax on your contributions to the scheme. The maximum contribution that you can make in any one year which qualifies for tax relief is related to your age. This is expressed as a percentage of your gross income. For example:

Age in year of contribution	Percentage of gross income for which tax relief is available
Under 30	15%
30-39	20%
40-49	25%
50-54	30%
55-59	35%
60 and over	40%

The above are just examples of the allowances that are available to you. In excess of €100 million of qualifying allowances go unclaimed by us each year, so make sure you know what you are entitled to and start claiming it. If in doubt, contact your local revenue office for clarification.

This is another form of saving for you and one that will not cost you a penny.

WHAT TO DO WITH YOUR SSIA SAVINGS

Between 1 May 2001 and 30 April 2002, 1.1 million Irish people decided to embark on a savings ritual never seen before, one that

would last for five years. I refer of course to the Special Savings
Investment Account or SSIA.

How many of the 1.1 million who opened SSIA accounts
would have done so were it not for the government's 25%
bonus? According to one leading bank that commissioned a
study amongst its new account holders, 76% of them were first-
time savers and 46% of these new accounts were opened to take
advantage of the government bonus.

The lump sums that many are now enjoying range from
€25,000 (depending on whether the account was deposit or equity
based) to just under €1,000. Most of this hard-saved cash is being
spent on the usual suspects:

* New cars
* Holidays
* Second property
* Home improvements
* Reducing mortgages
* Jewellery
* Home entertainment systems
* Clearing existing loans

A recent survey has indicated that more than one in eight people
will use the proceeds of their SSIA account to purchase a new
car. This will delight every dealership up and down the country,
but do you need to buy a '07 car? With this demand for new cars
many car dealers are likely to carry quite a number of trade-ins
and with new cars depreciating by up to 35% of their value in the
first two years, it may make financial sense to buy instead a car
that is only a couple of years old.

Rather than using all your SSIA money to purchase a new
car it might be prudent to use some of the money towards the
purchase – along with a possible trade-in – while financing the
remainder. You will have become used to a regular amount going
out each month anyway.

Back in 2001 and 2002 many people believed that at maturity a considerable amount of this SSIA money would be used by first-time buyers as a deposit to purchase their new homes and also by new investors to purchase a second property. For many years there have been a shortage of housing against demand, low interest rates, migration of a highly skilled workforce back into the country, increasing employment and an influx of workers from overseas. For all these reasons house prices in some areas have increased by incredible amounts over the past number of years. It is likely that the prospect of maturing SSIA money has also contributed to our spiralling house prices.

Many people are using the proceeds of their SSIAs to get on the elusive property ladder, and it has been a great incentive to first-time buyers in particular to use their savings as a deposit when buying a home for themselves. However, the introduction of a 100% mortgage facility means that first-time buyers may not have to use their savings as a deposit and if this is the case their savings can be put towards furnishing the property, or paying their legal fees for the purchase. The SSIA scheme gave first-time buyers encouragement and a fresh impetus to start saving; it also gave them direction, as they had to be dedicated and committed in saving each month to benefit from the scheme.

Those who are considering using their SSIA to purchase a property for investment for the first time should tread carefully. Be aware of a number of factors before you decide to embark on this project. First of all, a bank could require that you contribute up to 20% of the purchase price of the property. You will have to pay stamp duty, legal fees and furnish the property, register as a landlord and carry all the responsibility that come with it. For instance, on a property costing €350,000 the stamp duty alone is €21,000 – the value of one full SSIA account. Buying a property with your SSIA can be a very rewarding investment but before you commit to this course of action do your homework: know what your mortgage repayments will be; what your likely rental income will be; and whether you can afford the monthly repayment if the property is unoccupied for a couple of months.

Surveys carried out recently indicate that up to 50% of SSIA holders who plan to use their money on non-financial products will direct their spending to home improvements with extensions being high on their wish list. An extension, conservatory or a new kitchen may increase the value of your home but the reason many people decide on this plan is either that they need more space or feel it will improve their quality of life. Remember that what adds value to your home in your eyes and in the eyes of a potential buyer may be two different things; so take as much advice as possible before you decide on this course of action for this reason.

There is also a danger that with this type of demand, skilled building workers may be hard to come and prices will increase as a consequence – although the construction industry is at pains to assure us that this will not be the case.

I would encourage people – as mentioned in previous chapters – to clear their credit cards and high-interest-rate loans with the proceeds from their SSIA accounts, or use the funds to repay their mortgage more quickly.

What about putting your lump sum into a pension? The government has introduced an incentive to those who transfer up to €7,500 from their SSIA accounts into a new or existing pension fund within three months of their account maturing. Under the new initiative people will receive a bonus of €1 for every €3 they contribute, so those switching €7,500 from their SSIAs into a pension will receive a top up of €2,500.

This incentive was aimed at those on lower pay who are more likely to have inadequate pension arrangements. However, putting that money aside until retirement may be a hard decision for some people, and a lump sum of just €10,000 won't buy too big a pension in twenty years time, for example.

I know I sound like a stuck record but my advice is to hold some of that SSIA money back and put it into your EF! You know what it stands for!

With all this talk of what people are going to spend their 'windfall' on, the likelihood is that many people will reinvest some or all of their payout. This is borne out in a survey conducted by a leading financial institution, in which they found that 83% of their customers intended to save a portion of the money earned.

There are many many options to consider and people should take their time and weigh them up before deciding on a course of action. The banks cornered the SSIA market (would you believe they issued 93% of all SSIAs?) and they are all competing for your money. Do not let someone else make the decision for you as to where you should place your proceeds, and into what type of account. Get independent advice from a qualified financial adviser who will point out the products that are most suitable to your particular circumstances.

8

Protect Yourself and Your Family

This is a subject that many people do not like to talk about or deal with – and who can blame them? Death, serious illness and unemployment are not particularly pleasant subject matters. However, they are incredibly important. If you are the main breadwinner and you have children, think for a minute about their financial needs and those of your spouse if you were to die? Obviously you would not want the standard of living that they currently enjoy to drop in the event of your death or serious illness. By first understanding what effect death, serious illness, redundancy, an accident or illness would have on your dependants, you can make sure, by proper financial planning, that if the worst did happen your family would be well protected.

Let me ask you some questions:

- Do you have adequate life cover in place that would provide funds to replace your net monthly income in the event of your death?
- Do you even know how much cover you have?
- Do you know how much it should be?
- How much are you paying for the level of cover you have?
- What type of policy is it?
- Where is the policy document?
- Have you thought about what would happen if you suffered a serious illness?

- What happens if you had an accident and could not work for a number of months? How much would your current employer pay you and for how long?
- What would happen to your pension if you were to die?
- What would happen if your stay-at-home spouse died? Have you thought about childcare costs?
- How would you pay your mortgage and other bills if you had to live off a weekly disability benefit of just €200?

The main occurrences against which you need to have protection are:

- Death
- Serious illness
- Loss of income

First let's deal with life assurance.

HOW MUCH LIFE COVER DO YOU NEED?

This will very much depend on your own particular circumstances as one size does not fit all. Not everyone even needs life assurance. If you are single and have no dependants no one will be harmed financially by your death, so there is no real need for you to have life assurance. But if you are married and have children the financial impact of your death could be devastating to them, so the questions are: how much; and what type of policy is required?

I cannot stress enough that there is no general guideline that suits everyone. When I carry out reviews for new clients of mine and ask them how much cover they have, and why they have that amount, they tell me that when they took out the policy in the first place they were advised that it should be based on a multiple of their salary. What nonsense! All the following questions need to be answered in order to arrive at the amount of cover you need:

- What is your net monthly income, the
  income that needs to be replaced?
- What, if anything, will your spouse
  receive from your pension?
- What is the widow's state pension?
- Is there any investment income your spouse would
  continue to receive in the event of your death,
  for example rental income, share dividends?
- How much do you currently spend
  on yourself each month?
- How much are your mortgage repayments?
- How much do you pay for insurance?
- What is your existing level of life cover?
- How old are your children?
- Will your spouse be entitled to a death-in-service benefit?
- How much have you got in savings?

Below is an example of what I mean by factoring in the losses
and gains of income in death, so that you arrive at the correct
level of cover. The individual in question has a gross annual
salary of about €52,000 which equates to net monthly income of
about €3,500:

LIFE INSURANCE SUMMARY

If a fatal accident were to happen, his family would

Need to cover his monthly income of	€3,500
Less: monthly income payable on his death:	
Employer's pension	€0
Widow's state pension approximately (two dependent children)	€1,020
Investment income (rental income, share, dividends etc)	€0
Less: monthly income no longer required:	
Amount on self	€400
Mortgage repayment (covered by mortgage protection)	€1,000
Insurance repayments	€120
Monthly income required/shortfall	€960

To compensate fully for this change would require a lump sum of €384,000 less:

His existing level of life cover	€50,000
Death in service benefit if any	€0
Liquid assets - cashed within six months	€20,000
Which means that he would need additional life cover of	€314,000

So the individual's existing level of life cover, together with the new amount, and his savings when invested at a net rate of 3%, would generate a monthly income of €960 while maintaining the capital sum.

(The above is assuming that there are no other loans in place that need to be repaid in the event of the person's death. If, for example, you had a car loan and a personal loan that needed to be repaid you would increase the amount of cover in line with the amount outstanding on these loans.)

If this client had not reviewed the level of his life cover, his family would have been left in a serious financial situation in the event of his death. If he had worked off an income multiple of four times his salary he would have seriously underinsured himself, – 4 x €52,000 = €208,000, which is €106,000 short of what he should have had.

There will of course be cases where people are over-insured rather than under-insured. It is my experience, however, that the majority of us are under- rather than over-insured.

How Much Does It Cost?

The larger the sum assured, the higher your monthly premium will be. Other factors that influence the cost are:

* Age
* Smoker status
* Occupation
* Length of policy
* Current health status

Once you have decided on the right level of cover, is there really that much of a difference between the various life companies in the marketplace? You would be surprised!

Let's look at an example: we are looking for life cover in the amount of €200,000 level cover (stays the same amount) for a male aged forty-five next birthday, a non-smoker. The term of the policy is twenty years, with a convertible option (I will explain this option later in this chapter.).

Insurance Company	Monthly Premium
Life Company 1	€71.43
Life Company 2	€72.69
Life Company 3	€73.29
Life Company 4	€76.65
Life Company 5	€78.79
Life Company 6	€81.41
Life Company 7	€81.65

You can see from the above the difference from the cheapest and the dearest is €10.22 per month – a saving of €122.64 per annum.

Let's do the same example but this time we are going to include €50,000 worth of serious illness:

Insurance Company	Monthly Premium
Life Company 1	€101.15
Life Company 2	€110.99
Life Company 3	€112.41
Life Company 4	€112.45
Life Company 5	€129.01

As you can see from the above it is a worthwhile exercise to look for the cheapest life assurance available in the market, and if you do not have the time to do this yourself, get an independent financial adviser to do it for you.

SHOP AROUND

How many times, especially when we are organising a mortgage, do we let the lender arrange the life cover for us? More often than not it is done out of pure convenience on our part. You do realise that the lender will probably be operating as a tied agent, which means they can only arrange cover with one particular life company? Therefore you are getting no real choice. It is only when you read a book such as this or when you go to remortgage that you discover you were paying well over the odds.

Here is what you do, particularly if you are arranging life assurance for your mortgage. Well in advance, get a quote from your lender and from all the other assurance providers. Compare them, and if the benefits are more or less the same, pick the cheapest.

TYPES OF COVER

It is very important that you select the right type of life policy that is most suitable to you and your family. You want to ensure that it is the most competitive, and one that is paid quickly and easily to the beneficiaries of the policy.

These are the different types of policies that are available to you:

TERM ASSURANCE

This form of life cover insures you for the same amount throughout the agreed term.

Term assurance is ideal for people who know how much cover they need and for how long. For example, you can decide on the length of term that will cover your family right up until the youngest has left the family home to go to college, or begins to work and is financially independent. After that, the need for life cover will be much less.

At the end of the term of the policy the cover will stop and the policy finish. There is no surrender value attaching to this. It is advisable to have an option that allows you to increase the amount of cover if, for example, you have a second or third child. Your premiums will increase but having the flexibility to amend the level of cover is important.

Finally, when you take out a policy of this type you could structure it in such a way that if you were to die, the proceeds could be paid out very promptly to your spouse. If you take out a policy in your own name, you would be the life assured with your spouse being the owner of the policy. The proceeds would be paid directly to the owner rather than possibly being paid into your estate, where delays in payment might occur if, for instance, you had not made a will.

DECREASING LIFE COVER

This is also referred to as a mortgage protection policy and is a decreasing form of life assurance. If you elect to repay your mortgage by an interest and capital-type repayment, you know that part of your monthly repayment is going towards reducing some part of the original sum borrowed. You continue to make repayments until the mortgage has run its course and you no longer owe any money to your lender.

If you take out a mortgage protection policy to repay your mortgage on death, the life cover will reduce in line with the loan amount outstanding. Be aware, however, that any mortgage arrears are excluded.

The premiums for such a policy are fixed from the outset and although the life cover will reduce over time, the premium will not. At the end of the term nothing is payable and there is no surrender value. Due to the fact that the amount of cover reduces over time it is usually the cheapest form of cover.

This form of cover should be used only to protect your mortgage and you should not increase the sum assured, thinking you have additional cover if anything were to happen to you. Keep your mortgage protection and your other life assurance cover separate.

SERIOUS ILLNESS COVER

Most people do not realise that one out of every four men and one in five women will be diagnosed with a serious illness before they reach retirement age, including cancer, stroke, heart attack and a range of serious or chronic illnesses.

So if you or those who depend on you were to face financial hardship if you were diagnosed with a serious illness, it might be worth considering adding serious illness to either of the policies described above. If you become seriously ill, the last thing you want is any financial worry, such as the fear of losing your home because you cannot repay the mortgage. Having serious illness cover will give you peace of mind in these circumstances, as the policy will pay a benefit towards medical expenses and loss of income should a qualifying serious illness happen to you.

This kind of policy can be expensive, depending on the amount of cover required, and it is generally recommended that your level of cover should be at least twice your annual salary.

CONVERTIBLE OPTION

If you decide to include this option with your life policy it will mean that you can convert to another policy without giving further evidence of your state of health. If you have a young family and are on a tight budget, having this option may be a good idea. It will give you valuable options in later years if your income rises or your health declines.

MORTGAGE PAYMENTS PROTECTION

Mortgage payments protection, or home owner's payment protection, is a mortgage insurance policy whose aim is to cover your mortgage repayments in the event of redundancy, or your becoming ill and being unable to work for more than a specified period, normally one month. This type of insurance policy does not include death benefit. The policy should cover your monthly interest and capital repayments to your lender for a limited period, normally a maximum of twelve months. Obviously, if you are self-employed, the redundancy cover will not apply as you cannot make yourself redundant. However, if you are self-employed a hospitalisation benefit would apply, usually kicking in when you have been ten days in hospital.

If you have been out of work due to an illness, or were made redundant, you will know full well how fast a salary entitlement or redundancy payment runs out. Mortgage payments protection is designed to bridge this gap, so that you can concentrate on getting well, or on getting a new job. It will give you great peace of mind knowing that your mortgage repayments are protected, even for a period of twelve months.

The cost of your monthly premium will depend on the amount of the mortgage you want protected. The premium is based on a rate for every €100 of the mortgage repayment you wish to have covered. This cost is normally about €5 for every €100 you want covered.

Should a benefit become payable, the payment is made directly to the beneficiary's mortgage account. Where the payments protection is covering two borrowers, the same premium will apply. However, should one person claim, one of the following will apply: either 50% of the insured benefit is payable; or a portion of the benefit will be paid, based on the ratio of the income of the borrower who is making the claim to the total income of both borrowers.

There will be some restrictions to this cover, and for full details you should check the terms and conditions. You would be expected to be in full employment for a certain period of time to qualify for benefits under the redundancy section. You should not expect to be made redundant or have any expectation of unemployment within three months of going on cover. Other restrictions would include claims arising from pregnancy or child-birth, HIV-related illnessess, suicide or the wilful exposure to danger by the insured borrower, or any illness or disability the person applying for cover would have known of within one year prior to going on cover.

This form of cover can be expensive for what it is protecting you against, and I feel that is particularly useful to protect you against unemployment. If you are looking for protection against an illness or disability that prevents you from working, the following type of policy may be much more suitable.

INCOME PROTECTION

Have you ever asked yourself what would happen to your income if you were out of work for a long period of time? How long would your current employer pay your salary and how much of your salary would they pay? After that, how much benefit would you be entitled to? Many people do not know the answers to these questions. They ask the questions when it is too late, when they are out of work because of illness and realise that their employer will cover them only for a short period of time and that they have not made the necessary provisions to protect the shortfall.

Depending on your circumstances the disability benefit payable currently by the state can be as little as €180 per week. This is such a small amount to be in receipt of when mortgage repayments have to made, food purchased, bills paid, provisions made for children, transport provided and so on.

So what are you going to do about it, and what should you do first? Well, first of all, ask your employer how much of your salary they will pay, and for how long will they pay it, if you are out of work due to illness. Once you know this, you will be in a position to put in place a form of cover that replaces your lost income.

Permanent health insurance is a policy that provides an income payment if the insured person has 'suffered a loss of earned income due to being unable to follow his or her own occupation, or any other occupation for which he or she is reasonably suited or trained, due to sickness or disability lasting longer than a certain deferred period, and is not following any other occupation'.

It is important to note that incurring a loss of earned income is essential to qualify for the payment of the benefit.

Permanent health insurance (PHI) cover and serious illness cover are often mistaken for the same thing and can be confusing.

PHI cover pays you a regular income until such time you are ready to return to work, whereas serious illness cover pays out one lump sum in the event of your contracting a specified serious illness.

In order to ensure that an individual has an incentive to return to work, there are typically two main restrictions on the PHI cover provided: (a) cover may be restricted to 75% of earnings less any social welfare disability benefits and other ongoing income; and (b) there may be an overall monetary restriction on the cover provided, for example €75,000 per annum.

PHI premiums rates are very sensitive to the individual's occupation. Life companies tend to grade occupations in classes one to four. Occupations in Class 1 would tend to get normal rates whereas occupations in Class 4 might have rates twice the level of Class 1. There are some occupations that may not be offered PHI cover.

PHI premiums are normally tax deductible up to an annual limit of 10% of your income at your marginal rate of tax.

This kind of policy is extremely important for self-employed people who obviously do not have an employer to pay their salary if they are unable to work.

As regards cost, let's look at an example. Assume your salary is €50,000 and your occupation is deemed Class 1. You will need cover for €30,000 (€50,000 x 75% minus annual disability) with your retirement age at sixty. Your gross monthly premium would be €76.49, after tax relief €44.36.

(You can choose cover that remains level, or increases in line with inflation, and this will also have an effect on the cost.)

Not every life company offers this type of protection policy. You should seek independent advice from a qualified financial adviser who can compare the different premiums offered by the companies who do.

POINTS TO REMEMBER

When you are considering purchasing life assurance or any other form of protection remember to:

- Buy only the amount of life cover that is required to meet your family's needs in the event of your death.
- Shop around and compare prices – it may save you a lot of money.
- Get independent advice on the level of cover you require.
- Ask your employer how much they would pay you in the event of your being unable to work for a period of time.
- Review the amount of cover you have if you have not done so for a period of time.
- The younger you are when taking out cover, the cheaper the premiums will be.
- Put your policy document in a safe place.

9

FIFTY TIPS THAT WILL HELP TO SAVE YOU MONEY

1   KNOW YOUR MORTGAGE

This is probably your biggest debt, and it is one that many
people pay very little attention to. You have to know what
rate your current lender is charging you and find out how
competitive the rate is. If you are repaying at your lender's
standard variable rate, the chances are you are repaying
hundreds of euro each year more than you have to. For
example, the difference in monthly repayments, assuming a
loan amount of €300,000 over a thirty-year term, between a
standard variable rate of 4.99% and a tracker rate at 4.65%
from the same lender is €63 per month. This is a difference
of €756 each year!

2   SHOP AROUND FOR YOUR HOME INSURANCE

How much cover do you have for home insurance? How
much are you paying each month/year? Who is it with?
If you arranged your home insurance with your mortgage
provider then the chances are you are paying too much.

Get on-line and get some quotes. Use an independent
broker to do it for you if you don't have the time.
I did a review for a client of mine recently and I uncovered
that they were paying €576 per year for their home insurance
policy. For exactly the same cover I found a broker who
could arrange it at a cost of just €320 per year, saving them

€256 in the process.

3   Shop around for life assurance

Like home insurance, I believe it is important to find out how competitive your life assurance premiums are. When you arranged your mortgage with your bank or building society you are likely to have taken out a policy with them. Did they offer you any choice and cost comparisons? Of course not. So get going and find out if there there cheaper alternatives out there. You only have to look at the comparisons I did between a number of life companies in the previous chapter to see how much you can save.

4   How competitive is your car insurance?

You don't know? Well find out! Spend ten minutes on the phone or on-line and get a number of different quotes from the various providers. Let me give you an example of how premiums can differ from one company to another. A client of mine had a car valued at €19,000, was aged forty-six with a clean driving licence and had had a no-claims bonus for the previous five years. He shopped around and found that the cost of the annual premiums quoted by the different insurance companies varied from €320 right up to €550!

5   Get free holiday insurance

If you use your credit card to book your holiday on-line, you may get free travel insurance from your card provider for doing so.

6   Take advantage of credit card promotions

Switch to a a provider who offers 0% on balance transfers and your full monthly repayment will go towards eliminating your debt.

7   Forget the credit card and pay with cash

8   CUT YOUR TELEPHONE BILLS
There are alternatives to your current provider; check to
see who they are and how much their products cost. There
are serious savings to be made if you do. I checked on-
line recently and the difference between just two providers
amounted to €120 each year!

9   TAKE YOUR OWN LUNCH TO WORK FOR ONE WEEK EACH MONTH
By doing this you are going to save at least €50 each week,
or about €600 every year. Think of what you could do with
that money. In addition, you will probably enjoy your own
lunch more than the one you spend a fortune on each week.

10   QUIT SMOKING
Easier said than done, but it really is such an expensive
habit. If you were to get rid of that twenty-a-day you would
save yourself a whopping €2,500 a year. Try and cut back if
you can't give up altogether. Your health and finances will
greatly improve. By the way smokers pay up to 150% more
towards the cost of their life and serious-illness premiums
than non-smokers. Figures released recently show that a
non-smoker will pay €42.60 per month for life cover of
€300,000 over a twenty-five-year period, while a smoker
for the same amount of cover will pay €102.63 per month –
more than over €18,000 extra for the same amount of cover
over the twenty-five-year period.

11   CUT DOWN ON DRINKING
In this area drink-driving measures have helped enormously.
If you cut back a little at weekends you will also see your
finances improve. You can still go out and enjoy yourself;
just set a limit and stick to it.

12   CANCEL ANY CLUB MEMBERSHIP YOU DON'T USE
If you are not going to the gym at least twice a week or

playing golf at least twenty times each year at your golf
club cancel your membership immediately. A friend told me
recently that his annual gold membership last year was €800;
he played golf twice last year so each round effectively cost
him €400. Madness!

13   Cancel your digital TV
How many channels do you need? Do you really need ten
film channels and five sports channels? How often do you
watch them? I recently spoke to a couple who were having
money difficulties, and I noticed from their current account
statements that they were paying €90 each month for their
TV package. And they were wondering why they had money
problems!

14   Ensure that your current tax credits are
     correct and that you are claiming for all the
     benefits you are entitled to (See Chapter 7)

15   Get yourself a calendar and call it your bills reminder
Record on it what bills need to be paid every couple of
months and then plan accordingly.

16   Look after your health
Exercise and watch what you eat. If you do this now you
could avoid expensive medical bills in the future.

17   Cut down on those take-aways
Stop getting take-aways so often. Yes it's convenient, yes
you like the food but it is expensive if you are doing it two
or three times a week. Give yourself a take-away night once
a week. If you were to cut back on just one such meal each
week you would save yourself in the region of €1,000 per
year. Not to mention the benefits to your health!

18 TEACH YOUR CHILDREN THE VALUE OF SAVING
This will help them – and you –later in life when they won't
have to come back all the time to the Bank of Mum and Dad.
When they want you to buy them something, encourage
them to pay for it themselves with their own pocket money.

19 BEFORE BUYING A CAR CHECK WITH SEVERAL DEALERS
Get quotes from a number of different dealers so that you
can compare prices. Let each of them know that you are
doing this. You could save hundreds of euro.

20 SHOP AROUND FOR THE BEST CAR-FINANCE PACKAGE
Check with several lenders before you decide who you
are going to borrow the money from. Do not let the car
dealership arrange finance for you, that is, of course, unless
they have the best quote (unlikely, though).

21 DON'T ARRANGE FINANCE IN THE SHOP IN
WHICH YOU ARE BUYING AN ITEM
The rate of interest you will be charged is likely to be far
greater than if you were to borrow the money from your
local bank or credit union. Don't pay 16% when you could
pay 6% or 7%.

22 SWITCH TO A NO-FEES BANK FOR YOUR
CURRENT ACCOUNT REQUIREMENTS

23 AVOID PAYING LATE FEES ON CREDIT CARDS BY SETTING
UP A DIRECT DEBIT FROM YOUR ACCOUNT THAT WILL PAY
THE MINIMUM DUE OR THE FULL OUTSTANDING BALANCE

24 SHOP AT LOWER-PRICE FOOD STORES
You would save yourself hundreds of euro each year by
doing so.

25   MAKE A LIST WHEN YOU SHOP

You will spend less each week on food if you make a list and stick to it. If you don't know what you need, you will overspend.

26   EMPTY YOUR POCKETS EACH DAY AND PUT
     YOUR CHANGE IN A JAR OR MONEYBOX

27   BRING YOUR DVDS BACK ON TIME

28   GET AN 'APPROVAL IN PRINCIPLE' FOR YOUR MORTGAGE
     BEFORE YOU EVEN IDENTIFY A PROPERTY

It may strengthen your bargaining position with vendors and their auctioneers when you do find a suitable property.

29   TAKE ADVANTAGE OF THAT INCREASE
     IN YOUR PROPERTY'S VALUE

If you know that your home has increased in value, get it revalued and use the new figure to get your mortgage rate reduced. The lower the loan to value ratio, the cheaper the rate on offer.

30   RENT OUT A ROOM IN YOUR PROPERTY

If you have more space than you need, rent out a room and earn up to €7,620 each year tax free.

31   DON'T SHOP FOR FOOD WHEN YOU ARE TIRED OR HUNGRY

Research shows that you are likely to buy more sweets and food that are high in carbohydrates if you are tired or hungry.

32   BEWARE OF THE 'TWO FOR THE PRICE OF ONE' PROMOTION

You end up paying more for something that you really only need one of – that is unless you know you are going to use the two items.

33 DON'T RENEW YOUR SUBSCRIPTION TO NEWSPAPERS
    OR MAGAZINES IF YOU ARE NOT READING THEM

34 CHECK WHETHER YOUR MOTOR INSURANCE COMPANY
    WILL GIVE YOU A DISCOUNT IF YOU INSURE YOUR
    HOME WITH THEM ALSO (I BET THEY WILL)

35 KEEP YOUR LOAN REPAYMENTS UP TO DATE
    Failure to do so will result in you having a poor repayment
    record, and any further borrowing you may be sanctioned
    for will come at a higher than normal interest rate.

36 BUY A CAR THAT IS ONE OR TWO YEARS OLD
    You could get a car with 95% of its life left for 20–25% less
    than the cost of buying a brand-new car.

37 CUT DOWN ON THOSE CAPPUCCINOS
    One less each week will save you more than €150 each
    year.

38 COMPANY/ASSOCIATION PERKS
    Your company may have partners who offer special discounts
    or perks to employees. If you are a member of an affiliated
    body, check with them and see if you are entitled to any
    special offers. Some mortgage lenders will offer reduced
    rates to borrowers who have a particular qualification. Your
    company may even have a staff mortgage scheme, and you
    could be entitled to lower rates, no valuation fees (saving
    you €130), reduced legal fees and reduced home insurance
    premiums. If they don't have such a scheme, ask them to
    set one up.

39 BIN ANY PRE-APPROVED LOANS
    Next time you get a letter from your bank saying you have
    been pre-approved for a loan, don't even read it; bin it

immediately. This will remove your temptation to use it.

40   DRIVE SENSIBLY AND SAFELY
Don't accumulate penalty points because when the number
gets higher so will your insurance premiums.

41   BOOK FLIGHTS EARLY ON-LINE
You will save yourself a lot of money if you do. Check the
cost for each day in a particular month and find the lowest
price available.

42   AVAIL OF THE BEST CAR-HIRE OFFERS
If you need to hire a car abroad, book and pay on-line rather
than when you arrive at your destination. This is a highly
competitive market and discounts can be had.

43   USE PAY-AS-YOU-GO ON YOUR MOBILE PHONE
This may prove cheaper than a call plan, particularly if you
are a light user.

44   CAR POOL
Sharing the cost of getting to work each week with one or two
work colleagues will reduce fuel costs for all concerned.

45   BEWARE PAYMENTS PROTECTION
Don't take out a payments protection plan for your loan
from your bank if you don't need it. They are very profitable
for the banks, but very expensive for you.

46   MAKE OVERPAYMENTS ON YOUR MORTGAGE
By doing this you will reduce the term on your mortgage
and save yourself thousands of euro in interest. Use the
money you were putting towards your SSIA account against
your mortgage each month.

47 SHOP AROUND AND GET A BETTER RETURN ON YOUR SAVINGS

Ask an independent broker, or surf the net so that you can compare what is on offer out there. You may be earning 0.5% at present when you could be getting 4.5%

48 TOP UP YOUR CAR WHEN IT IS HALF FULL

Don't wait until the fuel light comes on in your car before you stop for fuel. Top it up when it is half-full. This will allow you to find the lowest price per litre available rather than having to top up out of necessity at a high-charging station.

49 CUT UP YOUR CREDIT CARD WHEN YOU HAVE
    EVENTUALLY REPAID THE AMOUNT OWING IN FULL

50 MARRY A MAN (OR WOMAN) WHO CAN FIX THINGS

It will save you thousands over the years. Thanks to my wife Roseann for this contribution.

10

Two Case Studies

In this chapter I will give you examples of real-life couples I have dealt with in the past and outline their situation before and after they got to grip with their finances. Maybe you have been in a similar situation and can learn from their experiences. (To protect privacy, names and details have been changed.)

Case Study Number 1: John and Jane

PROFILE

John is forty years old. He is employed in the services sector and has an annual income of €40,000. His wife, Jane, is thirty-eight, works in retail and has a salary of €25,000 per annum. They have two children aged eight and ten.

Their house is valued at €450,000 and they have an out-standing mortgage of €200,000. This is paid at their lender's variable rate of 4.99% and a twenty-five year term remains on it.

They have no savings at the moment.

John is highly valued by his employer and will be paid his full salary for three months if he is out of work because of illness or injury.

Jane's employer will not pay her at all should she be out of work.

Their mortgage is protected by a life assurance policy and they have one other policy in John's name which would pay Jane a benefit of €150,000 on his death.

They have two unsecured loans in place at present, a car loan and a personal/holiday loan. They have one credit card each, with about €10,000 outstanding between the two.

They have no pension provisions in place at present.

They had no idea how much their home was insured for, or how much they were paying each month, but I quickly discovered that they were paying €60 each month.

Their concerns are that they have no money left in their account any month and as a result have been using their credit cards more and more often to purchase their groceries and Christmas gifts. Their car will need to be changed soon and the children are asking when they will be going on a holiday abroad.

They cannot understand why they are in such a predicament when: (a) they don't go out much; (b) they don't drive a flash car and; c) think their income is reasonably good. They are in a rut and just don't know where to start.

The first thing we need to look at is a summary of their monthly cashflow:

Income from Employment	Per Month
John	€2,600
Jane	€1,800
Other Regular Sources of Income	
Children's Allowance	€300
Total Net Monthly Income	€4,700

Fixed Expenses	Per Month
Mortgage	€1,170
Car Loan	€450
Holiday Loan	€270
Credit Cards	€400
Mortgage Protection	€90
Life Assurance (John)	€60
Health Insurance	€120
Car Insurance	€50
Home Insurance	€60
Total Fixed Monthly Expenses	€2,670

Variable Expenses	Per Month
Food Shopping	€650
Eating out/Take-aways (twice weekly at €30)	€260
Lunches	€325
Smoking (John x 15 each day)	€145
Petrol	€150
Satellite TV	€60
Children's Pocket Money (€10 x 2 each week)	€87
Top up Phone Credit	€100
Clothing	€150
Entertainment/Sports/Leisure	€150
Newspapers/Magazines	€20
Savings	€0
Pension	€0
Gas/Electricity/Phone (average per month)	€400
Total Variable Monthly Expenses	€2,497

SUMMARY

Income	Outgoings
€4,700	€5,167

No wonder they were in trouble: each month they were spending €467 more than what they were earning. Rather than targeting everything from the word go, I started gradually. I identified three areas from their fixed expenses and three from their variable expenses where they could immediately save money without it being too painful.

The areas I decided to focus on were:

FIXED EXPENSES

- Mortgage
- Car loan
- Mortgage protection policy

VARIABLE EXPENSES

- Food
- Take-aways
- Lunches

MORTGAGE

Their current mortgage was paid at a rate of 4.99%. Given that the value of their property was €450,000 and their loan was just €200,000, it meant that the bank's exposure here was just 44% (loan to value ratio).

We contacted their bank and asked them for their current mortgage rates. We told the bank the value of their property and said that if they did not reduce their rate immediately we would move their mortgage to another lender who would pay their legal fees for moving. Lo and behold the bank had a rate of 4.25% on offer for those with a loan to value of less than 80%.

The difference in repayments between the two rates was €84 per month, so this is our first saving. (By the way, this took about thirty minutes to achieve.)

Saving number 1: €84 per month.

CAR LOAN

John had arranged his car finance with his local bank. He was paying €400 each month with four years remaining on the loan.

We went on-line and secured a monthly repayment of €364 (the same amount, just at a cheaper rate). It wasn't with his existing bank but who cares.

Saving number 2: €36 per month.

MORTGAGE PROTECTION POLICY

I noticed from their policy schedule that the type of cover was 'level term', which means that the amount of cover remains the same all the time. However, their mortgage was repaid on an interest-and-capital basis, so their mortgage was reducing each month. Why then did they have a level term policy? They had no idea; the bank had arranged it for them and they did not know what decreasing or level cover meant anyway. So they were paying €90 per month for a policy that really should only be costing them €52. We cancelled that policy when we had replaced it with another and this was Saving Number 3: €38 per month.

By looking at just three fixed outgoings I was able to reduce their outgoings by €158 each month in a very short space of time.

VARIABLE EXPENSES

On to their variable expenses, which are obviously harder for me to control. John and Jane have to be committed to reducing their spending and changing their habits.

When we looked at their current account statements over the previous few months and they realised how much they were spending in some of the categories outlined above they could not believe it. They were asking themselves, for example, how were they spending €650 each month on groceries for the four of them? Were lunches really costing them €325 every month? Surely not? Only two take-aways each week! Yes, but at €25 a time!

GROCERIES

We gave John and Jane a weekly budget of €120 for their grocery shopping. They were to make a list of what they needed and when they went shopping they were to pay in cash, so they could not go above this figure.

They were to go to other shops to compare prices because they only ever shopped in one store. I wanted them not just to look at food prices, but at household cleaning products and healthcare products.

They didn't change where they bought most of their items, but became very conscious of what they were spending their money on. They made lists and stuck to them and after a month they had saved €80.

TAKE-AWAYS

They decided that they would continue to have a take-away meal one night each week and decided that this night was going to be Thursday.

No matter how much they wanted a second take-away they were not going to get it; they would instead prepare meals in advance.

By doing this they were going to save a whopping €130 each month.

LUNCHES

I suggested to John and Jane that during one week each month they would bring their own lunch to work. I asked them to put the amount they would have spent on sandwiches and coffees – €15 each day – into a jar.

At the end of the week there was €75 in the jar. It is not rocket science and you know €15 by 5 is €75 but sometimes it will only dawn on you when you see the money there in the jar.

I think this is a great exercise to concentrate the mind on saving money: continue to withdraw the amount you would have spent, but put it away in a drawer or jar, so that you can then hold the savings in your hand.

Another €75 saved each month.

SUMMARY POST-CUTBACKS/REDUCTIONS

Income	Outgoings
€4,700	€4,724

In the first month, we were able to save €443 in these six expenses alone. Instead of living in their overdraft or paying for things with their credit card, John and Jane were now at break-even point.

Their life had not changed dramatically. They were still eating out, still having a good time, but they had just started to cut back a little, become conscious of what they were spending their money on, become focused on getting better value for their money, started to compare other products against what they had been paying and set themselves a budget each month.

The reasons John and Jane were in a cashflow mess in the first place were:

- Overspending
- Poor advice
- Not setting budgets
- No planning
- Not monitoring their account more regularly or knowing when repayments were debited from their account

Break-even is a good start but John and Jane have other areas that they need to address urgently:

- They need to build an emergency savings fund.
- John is seriously underinsured in the event of
  his death and the existing life cover pay-out to
  Jane would last only for three to five years.
- What happens if John is out of work
  for longer than three months?
- When are they going to be able to start a pension?

All the above come at a cost, and they cannot start addressing these problems if they do not have the funds to do so. They have to prioritise which of the above is most important to them now and get that in place first. Then, as their disposable income increases, they can start a pension or savings plan, or whatever they decide is most appropriate for them.

I remember at one meeting John saying to Jane, 'Think what we could do with that credit card repayment.' An awful lot was the answer. They could probably put all those things in place – life cover, income protection, pension – with that amount of money. So, they are going to look at cutting back even more.

For instance, John's smoking habit is costing them €145 per month. I told John this is what he can get for the amount he spends on cigarettes each month:

- An extra €200,000 worth of life cover so
  his wife and children are financially secure
  in the event of his death (€36 p/m)
- 75% of his income protected in the event of him being
  unable to work due to an accident or illness (€57 p/m)
- He could start a savings plan for €52
  each month with the remainder.

When you show someone what they can get for the amount they are spending on cigarettes (ten to fifteen a day) it quickly focuses the mind and puts things into perspective. I told him to think of this every time he lights up from now on.

After the initial month we agreed that our plan of action would include the following:

- John was to set up a deduction of €50 from his salary each month to go into a new savings account.
- The couple was to keep a diary of what they spent their money on.
- They were to set a budget each month and not exceed it.
- They were to monitor what was in their account every second day.
- They were to change the repayment dates on their fixed monthly outgoings so that they all went out in one lump sum soon after they are both paid.
- They were to switch their credit card to a 0% on balance transfers provider and continue with the €400 payment each month. After six months their balance will have reduced by a full €2,400. If, at the end of that free term, they cannot switch to another provider offering the same 0%, we will get a term loan from a bank at a cheaper rate to clear the credit card debt.
- John was to try to give up smoking and use this saving towards purchasing more life cover and income protection.

I asked them to find out what exactly they were entitled to claim back on their tax bill. It might be nothing, but at least it was getting them into the habit of asking questions.

John and Jane did implement the above and now have got to the stage that they don't need to monitor their account every other day; they are not worried about increasing interest rates; they do 'shop around' every six months to make sure they are still getting the best deals possible; they don't dread that 'financial review'; and they tell me they are much much happier.

They still don't have everything in place and that credit card is still not cleared. But they know the exact date it will be cleared and for the first time in a long time they have some money in their account.

CASE STUDY NUMBER 2: MARK AND AISLING

PROFILE

Mark is thirty-seven years old and is self-employed. His annual income is €40,000. His wife, Aisling, is thirty-four, and has been out of work for the past four years following an illness. She is in receipt of a disability benefit of €202 per week. They have two children aged six and two.

Their house is valued at €300,000 and they have an outstanding mortgage of €140,000. This is paid at their lender's variable rate of 4.85% and they have a twenty-five-year term remaining.

They have €10,000 in savings with their local credit union, as they received a gift from Mark's parents a couple of years ago.

Their mortgage is protected by a life assurance policy and they have one other policy in joint names covering Mark's life in the amount of €150,000 and Aisling's for €120,000.

They have four unsecured loans in place at present, which are detailed as:

Lender	Amount Outstanding	Monthly Repayment	Purpose of Loan
Leasing Company	€5,000	€155	Car Loan
Credit Union	€5,600	€125	Holiday Loan
Credit Union	€14,000	€600	Home Improvement
Visa Card	€9,000	€315	Miscellaneous

Mark is contributing €130 towards a pension plan at present but has no idea as to the value of the pension funds or how much he will receive when he retires.

Their monthly mortgage repayment has increased over the past twelve months as a result of interest-rate increases and they are currently repaying €840 per month.

SUMMARY

Their total net monthly income is €3,805.

Fixed Outgoings	Per Month
Mortgage	€840
Car Loan	€155
Credit Union Loans x 2	€725
Credit Card	€315
Mortgage Protection	€22
Life Assurance	€40
Home Insurance	€36
Health Insurance	€102
Car Insurance	€45
Pension	€130
Total	€2,410

This leaves them with €1,400 towards their variable expenses each month, or €325 each week.

Aisling is great when it comes to money management and can stretch that sum each month but there are times when she has to use her credit card to purchase groceries or cover school expenses. The couple does not go out very often and they are very conscious of what they spend their money on. They have to, because they know exactly how much is left after all the loans and insurance premiums are paid. Aisling looks for bargains, gets books from the library for her children rather than buying them, puts a little bit away each week which will be used for Christmas but Mark is unaware that she does this.

Aisling is the accountant of the family and knows all there is to know about their finances. Mark doesn't know and does not want to know. The problem with this couple is not overspending or poor money management. Aisling is, as I said, superb at managing money. Their problem is that not enough money is coming in to service the debt they have accumulated over the years and their worry is that because they are so reliant on Mark's income they would be in serious trouble if anything happened to him that prevented him working for a period of time – they have experience of this with what happened to Aisling.

Debt Consolidation

The answer to this couple's problems is debt consolidation. If we consolidate all their loans and existing mortgage into one – €173,600, secured on their family home – their fixed monthly repayments over a twenty-five year term would look like this:

Lender	Rate	Monthly Repayment
Mortgage Company	4.25%	€940.90

SUMMARY POST-CONSOLIDATION

If they consolidate all their loans into one, their fixed expenses will now look like this:

Mortgage	€941
Mortgage Protection	€30
Life Assurance	€40
Home Insurance	€36
Health Insurance	€102
Car Insurance	€45
Pension	€130
Total	€1,324

If they do this, their cashflow is going to improve by a whopping €1,086 per month. This will give them an extra €250 each week that can now be directed towards:

- An income protection plan for Mark which will cover him for 75% of his income should he be out of work due to an accident or illness. This will cost him €75 per month but he can now afford to pay it.
- Increasing Mark's life cover by €100,000 as he was under-protected previously. This will cost the couple €15 per month.
- Increasing Mark's pension contributions by €100 each month
- Starting a savings plan of €100 each month
- Mortgage overpayment of €100 each month

All the above will cost them €390 per month and they obviously could not afford to finance this prior to their consolidation loan.

They still have €696 each month more they had before and now they have peace of mind knowing that Mark's income is protected; he has adequate life cover in place; he is building an excellent pension fund for them when they retire; and they are adding to their existing savings.

There is no point in remortgaging or consolidating all your loans into one smaller repayment unless you are going to do something with that money. Good financial planning should accompany any decision to consolidate. Whenever I arrange this type of loan for clients, I identify with them what we are going to spend some of that spare cash on.

I suggested to Mark and Aisling that with the extra money they overpay their mortgage by €100 each month, which at first they thought a bit odd, but by doing this they will reduce the term on their mortgage by three years nine months, saving along the way more than €19,000 in interest payments. They still have nearly €600 in surplus income after doing this.

Remember that by spreading short-term debt over a longer period you end up paying more in interest repayments and you convert unsecured debt into secured debt. But as long as you are aware of what you are undertaking, the decision is yours. In Mark and Aisling's case it is more important for them to increase their cashflow each month than worry about how much more interest they will be repaying, but each individual will have different priorities. Just make sure you get advice from a qualified professional who is not just concerned about getting your remortgage done as quickly as possible, but is keen to look at the bigger picture for you and your family.

11

KNOWING WHEN YOU ARE IN TOO DEEP

TIME TO SEEK HELP

There are some people whose level of debt has got to the stage that, no matter how much they cut back and watch what they spend their money on and no matter how closely they monitor their account, their debt continues to rise or, worse still, they start missing monthly loan commitments. This may be a good time to admit that you have a problem, one that you are are incapable of solving yourself, and it may be time to seek professional help.

If any of the below happening frequently to you, debt advice or debt counselling is a course of action you should consider:

- You are juggling or even ignoring bills until you start getting final reminders.
- You are receiving phone calls at home or letters from finance companies about arrears on your account.
- You are using your credit card more frequently to buy food and petrol.
- You are hiding the true level of your accumulated debt from your spouse.
- You are constantly living in your overdraft.
- Christmas and birthdays are not as happy as you would like them to be because you worry about how you are going to pay for gifts, or how you are going to pay back the money borrowed to buy them.
- You think about your financial predicament 24/7.

- You are looking for new credit but have been
  refused because of a poor credit history.

It does not matter if your debt is €1,000 or €50,000: what matters is the income you have each month, what your outgoings are, and what you would like your financial future to be.

If you feel that you just can't get a handle on your finances and this is affecting your quality of life, seek help. Here in Ireland the Money Advice and Budgeting Service, MABS for short, is a national service available to people in debt and is free and confidential. MABS have offices nationwide and it may be in your best interest to get help from them.

CREDIT CHECK YOURSELF

When you apply for any form of finance, the lending institution will do a check on you with the Irish Credit Bureau to ensure that you have never been bankrupt or had judgements registered against you. They will view your repayment history on previous loans. This is a very important procedure for lenders, as it allows them to view how you conducted the repayment of previous loans, whether you were ever in arrears and, if so, by how many months.

Sometimes people apply for a loan and, while their ability to repay the loan is without question, they are refused finance because of a poor credit bureau record. It can be very frustrating, as you may not remember loans you had in the past and, if you do remember, you think your repayment record was OK. (What you think is OK and what a lender thinks could be two different things.) A lender will frown upon repeated unpaids or a pattern of missed monthly repayments. What a lender sees on the bureau record will not tell them why the repayments were missed, just that they were.

It is possible to get bad credit details removed or amended if the details recorded are incorrect. However, if you failed to repay a loan on time, or if you did not keep to the terms of the loan agreement, the lender will not amend your credit rating. Remember too that it is only the financial institution with which you had the loan that has the power to amend your repayment profile.

If you are acting as a guarantor for a loan, be aware that if the person you are helping fails to meet repayments on time or fails to repay the loan eventually, it will reflect on you and the loan profile will be recorded under your name as well.

In July 2004 providers of credit cards were given the option to supply information on credit card repayments and they can reveal if they ever cancelled or revoked cards held by individuals. Credit Unions have also been invited to join the bureau, of which there are currently thirty-eight members. Loans recorded with the bureau will continue to appear on your record for a period of five years from the date the loan was completed.

If you are in any doubt at all about any previous loans you may have held, why don't you credit-check yourself and look at exactly what every lender will see when you are applying for a new facility. A fee of €6 together with a completed request form (available from the Irish Credit Bureau's website) should be sent to the bureau, which will then forward to you the results of their credit search on you.

I cannot stress too much the importance of having a good repayment record, as it has significant bearing on whether lending institutions will advance funds to you. So whether it is a mortgage, a car loan or how you operate your credit card, make sure you meet the repayments on time. This will, of course, come from good planning and management of the account from which your monthly commitments are debited.

Behind with Mortgage Repayments – What to Do

If you miss one, two, or more mortgage repayments with your lender, arrears will obviously build up on your mortgage account. You could be liable for interest penalties as a result of being in arrears since you have failed to honour your commitment to the mortgage agreement. This arrears charge will be added to your account each month and charges can accumulate to such an extent that the penalties alone are significant in size.

Nobody wants to go into arrears. Arrears on mortgages happen for a variety of reasons, from bad management of your finances each month to being made redundant, or being unable to work for a period of time due to an accident or serious illness.

Lending institutions are very conscious of the mortgages held with them that go into arrears. Some institutions will have a dedicated team whose job it is to monitor and identify loans which they feel need attention, to avoid the risk of borrowers eventually defaulting altogether on the loan repayments. So if, for whatever reason, you are finding it difficult at the moment to make your mortgage repayment, the first thing you should do is contact your mortgage lender and advise them of your current predicament and circumstances.

A lender will welcome the fact that you are bringing this problem to their attention and will endeavour to work with you to help overcome your difficulties both in the short and long term. Their last resort will be to seek a court order to repossess your property, so if you talk with your lender, work with them and honour the solution you agree to, you will be fine.

On a personal level you have to deal with this issue from the word go. Do not ignore the problem and if you feel you cannot deal with the problem yourself, approach someone who will agree to speak to the lender and negotiate on your behalf. Failing to address the situation will make matters a whole lot worse for you in the long run.

To reduce your repayment burden some lenders may be prepared to offer you, for example, a moratorium on your mortgage repayments. This means that you do not make a full monthly repayment but do agree to the repayment of a notional amount – an amount varying from lender to lender that may range from €1 to €100 per month. You will, however, have to continue with the full repayment of your life and home insurance premiums. The moratorium may last for a limited period and the missed repayments – or the difference between what you are repaying and what you should be repaying – are added to the amount you owe on the mortgage.

Another solution a lender may suggest is extending the term of your mortgage. Would an extension of ten years on your mortgage reduce your monthly repayment to an amount that is more manageable?

If you were two or three months in arrears on your mortgage account and have been paying the full instalment without difficulty for some time now, but just cannot find that extra sum each month to reduce the arrears by any reasonable amount, your lender may suggest cleaning the slate and adding the arrears on to the amount you currently owe. You will then be starting afresh with no arrears and you will feel much better about it. But be aware that by doing this you are effectively capitalising your arrears and increasing the amount you owe upon which interest is charged. You are going to be repaying those missed months over a much longer period, maybe fifteen or even twenty years. You will also have to increase your life assurance to cover the amount added to your mortgage account, but regardless of these disadvantages, it might be the option which best suits your present circumstances.

Your lender may also agree to interest-only repayments whereby you service only the interest portion of your loan. The difference in repayments between this and an interest-and-capital method of repayment could be significant and help you overcome your difficulties.

I cannot stress too much the importance of communicating with your lender if you are in arrears, or fear you are going to be, so that you can explore with your lender what options are available to you and work out a solution that suits you both.

12

OUT OF THE RED AND INTO THE BLACK

If you follow the recommendations I have made throughout this book, I have no doubt that you can get to grips with managing and spending your money much more effectively than ever before.

KNOW YOUR MONEY

It starts with knowing how much money is coming in and where it is going. You have to make a commitment to the changes you are going to implement and stick with them. Over a short space of time your attitude to money will change and you will see a noticeable improvement in your finances. It is best to keep your financial plans simple but you have to work at it and spend some time figuring out where you currently are and where you want to be.

Start taking control of your hard-earned money: know what is coming in and going out; keep a record of what you are spending your money on; start making phone calls to check how competitive your existing finance arrangements are. These may not be enjoyable tasks for some people but I guarantee you that you will reap the benefits.

Organise your bank statements, insurance documents and monthly bills in a file or ring binder. If you are organised, so too will your finances be.

List your financial objectives under short and long-term goals. The list may be something like this:

SHORT TERM

- Clear credit cards
- Open a savings account
- Build an emergency fund

LONG TERM

You may want to:

- Retire at 55
- Buy a holiday home abroad
- Add a conservatory to your home

And so on.

Set objectives that are achievable. Maybe clearing your credit card debt is a long-term rather than short-term goal. There is no point in having goals that you have little chance of reaching.

SHOP AROUND

I want you to carry our this exercise as soon as possible; you will need to set aside twenty minutes each day for one week to complete these tasks.

MONDAY

Call your mortgage provider and find out the rate at which you are currently repaying your mortgage. If it is a standard variable rate ask what their tracker rate is and if it is cheaper, say you want to switch to it immediately.

Go on-line and check other lenders' rates and see if there are cheaper rates to be had. Forget loyalty!

TUESDAY

Call a general insurance broker, give them your home insurance details and ask them if they can get the same cover for you at a cheaper price.

Wednesday

Contact an independent life-assurance broker and check with them that your current life and mortgage protection premiums are the best available in the marketplace.

Thursday

Go on-line and see if your current car loan repayments are up to scratch.

Friday

Get an application form from a credit card provider that offers 0% on balance transfers and transfer your balance to them. For the next six or nine repayments your full monthly repayment will go towards reducing the amount outstanding. Remember not to use this credit card for purchases; in fact you should cut it up as soon as you receive it.

The following week you could carry out the same exercise on your car insurance, phone provider and health insurance provider.

Be proactive. Do not take anything for granted and do not assume that all your borrowings are at the best rates you could possibly get. None of the above exercises will take much time and they are likely to save you thousands of euro each year. If you do not make any savings, at least you will know that the financial products you have are well priced and that you are getting value for your money.

I would urge you to put your plan and budgets on paper; in that way they are easier to keep track of and you are more likely to stick to them. Buy yourself an extra calendar, put it up in the kitchen, record on it when two-monthly bills arrive, or when once-off yearly payments are due. Plan for these payments accordingly.

Get your children into the savings habit. Open a new account for them, encourage them and reward them when their savings reach a certain limit.

GOOD HOUSEKEEPING

- Total your expenses each week in the various different spending categories and compare how you are doing against your monthly budget.

- Monitor the balance in your account at least twice a week.

- If there is any surplus money in your account at the end of the month put it into a savings account.

- If you are self-employed set money aside each month for your annual tax bill.

- Pay the bills due each month on time.

- Know what your fixed loan commitments are and when they are debited from your account.

- Plan well in advance for any major purchases for the forthcoming year, for example Christmas, holidays and home improvements.

- Get a financial review carried out once a year by an independent financial adviser.

- Don't spend what you don't have.

- Budget for paying a minimum fixed amount each month on your credit cards and don't get sucked into the minimum payment trap.

- Monitor your savings regularly and make sure you are getting the best return for the money you have on deposit.

If you want to move from the red to the black start paying more attention to what you are spending your money on. Get focused and plan for your short- and long-term goals; be aware of other products in the marketplace that may be better priced than what you currently have; alter your shopping habits; get advice if you need it. All these will lead to a significant improvement in your finances and ultimately to your financial wellbeing and that of your family. Only you can make it happen: make a commitment, get out pen and paper and start planning now.